A HUMAN
PATTERN

SELECTED POEMS

Judith Wright: A Select Bibliography

POETRY
The Moving Image (1946)
Woman to Man (1949)
The Gateway (1953)
The Two Fires (1955)
Birds: Poems (1962)
Selected Poems (1963)
The Other Half (1966)
Collected Poems 1941 - 76 (1971)
Alive, Poems 1971 - 72 (1973)
Fourth Quarter and Other Poems (1976)
The Double Tree: Selected Poems 1942 - 76 (1978)
Phantom Dwelling (1985)

PROSE
The Generations of Men (family history) (1959)
The Nature of Love (short stories) 1966
Preoccupations in Australian Poetry (1965)
Because I Was Invited (essays) (1975)
The Coral Battleground (documentary on the conservation question and political action) (1977)
We Call for a Treaty (political and historical survey) (1985)

A HUMAN
PATTERN

Judith Wright

SELECTED POEMS

A division of HarperCollins*Publishers*

AN ANGUS & ROBERTSON BOOK

First published in Australia by Angus & Robertson Publishers in 1990
This edition published by Collins/Angus & Robertson
Publishers Australia in 1990
Reprinted in 1990

Collins/Angus & Robertson Publishers Australia
A division of HarperCollinsPublishers (Australia) Pty Limited
Unit 4, Eden Park, 31 Waterloo Road, North Ryde
NSW 2113, Australia

William Collins Publishers Ltd
31 View Road, Glenfield, Auckland 10, New Zealand

Angus & Robertson (UK)
16 Golden Square, London W1R 4BN, United Kingdom

National Library of Australia
Cataloguing-in-Publication data:

Wright, Judith, 1915–
    A human pattern.

    ISBN 0 207 16484 3
    1. Title.

A821.3

Cover painting: PARROTS *by Sylvana Gardner*
Typeset in Hong Kong by Best-set Typesetter Ltd
Printed in Australia by Griffin Press

 6   5   4   3
95 94 93 92 91 90

FOREWORD

For many years, a notion has been around that poetry is dying, if not dead. It hasn't died, and unless a dislike generated in school and university days prevails, it won't die.

But it is certainly in danger, just as the earth itself is in danger, from the philosophies generated by greed. Materialism, positivism and behaviourism are foes of both poetry and the survival of the earth. They have ruled during my lifetime; but I think they are on the way out.

Poems, like all literature, are written from within a social, historical and personal context and bearing. The poems in this selection emerged from my own life, from the early days of World War II when fear, loss, displacement and destruction filled lives in Australia as elsewhere, to today when we are in even greater peril of losing the very world we live in, through the results of ignorance, greed and immensely increased power. These poems were written in these times and, along with my own search for wholeness, their themes are dominated by the way I saw those influences.

And the plight of the peoples who had lived here before us for so many thousands of years, and whose care for this country left us the fertility and beauty our times are now laying waste, runs as an undercurrent through the book.

I think poetry should be treated, not as a lofty art separated from life, but as a way of seeing and expressing not just the personal view, but the whole context of the writer's times. For me, it has been a way of searching for understanding of my own life and of what was happening to me and around me.

Judith Wright
1989

CONTENTS

FROM
THE MOVING IMAGE

The Company of Lovers

We meet and part now over all the world;
we, the lost company,
take hands together in the night, forget
the night in our brief happiness, silently.
We, who sought many things, throw all away
for this one thing, one only,
remembering that in the narrow grave
we shall be lonely.

Death marshals up his armies round us now.
Their footsteps crowd too near.
Lock your warm hand above the chilling heart
and for a time I live without my fear.
Grope in the night to find me and embrace,
for the dark preludes of the drums begin,
and round us, round the company of lovers,
death draws his cordons in.

Bora Ring

The song is gone; the dance
is secret with the dancers in the earth,
the ritual useless, and the tribal story
lost in an alien tale.

Only the grass stands up
to mark the dancing-ring; the apple-gums
posture and mime a past corroboree,
murmur a broken chant.

The hunter is gone; the spear
is splintered underground, the painted bodies

a dream the world breathed sleeping and forgot.
The nomad feet are still.

Only the rider's heart
halts at a sightless shadow, an unsaid word
that fastens in the blood the ancient curse,
the fear as old as Cain.

Blue Arab

The small blue Arab stallion dances on the hill
like a glancing breaker, like a storm rearing in the sky.
In his prick-ears the wind, that wanderer and spy,
sings of the dunes of Arabia, lion-coloured, still.

The small blue stallion poses like a centaur-god,
netting the sun in his sea-spray mane, forgetting
his stalwart mares for a phantom galloping unshod;
changing for a heat-mirage his tall and velvet hill.

Trapped Dingo

So here, twisted in steel, and spoiled with red
your sunlight hide, smelling of death and fear,
they crushed out of your throat the terrible song
you sang in the dark ranges. With what crying
you mourned him!—the drinker of blood, the swift
    death-bringer
who ran with you many a night; and the night was long.
I heard you, desperate poet. Did you hear
my silent voice take up the cry?—replying:
Achilles is overcome, and Hector dead,
and clay stops many a warrior's mouth, wild singer.

Voice from the hills and the river drunken with rain,
for your lament the long night was too brief.
Hurling your woes at the moon, that old cleaned bone,
till the white shorn mobs of stars on the hill of the sky
huddled and trembled, you tolled him, the rebel one.
Insane Andromache, pacing your towers alone,
death ends the verse you chanted; here you lie.
The lover, the maker of elegies is slain,
and veiled with blood her body's stealthy sun.

Remittance Man

The spendthrift, disinherited and graceless,
accepted his pittance with an easy air,
only surprised he could escape so simply
from the pheasant-shooting and the aunts in the close;
took to the life, dropped easily out of knowledge,
and tramping the backtracks in the summer haze
let everything but life slip through his fingers.

Blue blowing smoke of twigs from the noon fire,
red blowing dust of roads where the teams go slow,
sparse swinging shadow of trees no longer foreign
silted the memory of a greener climate.
The crazy tales, the hatters' crazy secrets,
the blind-drunk sprees indifferently forgiven,
and past them all, the track to escape and nowhere
suited his book, the freak who could never settle.
That pale stalk of a wench at the county ball
sank back forgotten in black Mary's eyes,
and past the sallow circle of the plains' horizon
faded the rainy elms seen through the nursery window.

That harsh biblical country of the scapegoat
closed its magnificence finally round his bones
polished by diligent ants. The squire his brother,

presuming death, sighed over the documents,
and lifting his eyes across the inherited garden
let a vague pity blur the formal roses.

Soldier's Farm

This ploughland vapoured with the dust of dreams,
these delicate gatherings of dancing trees,
answered the question of his searching eyes
as his wife's body answered to his arms.

He let the whole gold day pass in a stare,
walking the turning furrow. The horses drew
his line straight where the shakesword corn should grow.
He, lurching mooncalf, let his eyes stride far.

They stooped across the swell and sink of hill;
made record of the leaves that played with light.
The mist was early and the moon was late,
and in between he stared his whole day full.

He asked for nothing but the luck to live,
so now his willing blood moves in these trees
that hold his heart up sunwards with their arms.
The mists dissolve at morning like his dreams
and the creek answers light as once his eyes;
and yet he left here nothing but his love.

The Trains

Tunnelling through the night, the trains pass
in a splendour of power, with a sound like thunder
shaking the orchards, waking

the young from a dream, scattering like glass
the old men's sleep, laying
a black trail over the still bloom of the orchards;
the trains go north with guns.

Strange primitive piece of flesh, the heart laid quiet
hearing their cry pierce through its thin-walled cave
recalls the forgotten tiger,
and leaps awake in its old panic riot;
and how shall mind be sober,
since blood's red thread still binds us fast in history?
Tiger, you walk through all our past and future,
troubling the children's sleep; laying
a reeking trail across our dream of orchards.

Racing on iron errands, the trains go by,
and over the white acres of our orchards
hurl their wild summoning cry, their animal cry . . .
the trains go north with guns.

The Idler

The treasure islands were his desired landfall:
past the grey discipline of streets and past
the minatory towers with their clocks
the sails rose bannering on the saltwhite mast.
The islands ran like emeralds through his fingers
(Oparo, Manahiki, Tubuai)
till he turned truant, cleared the heads at dawn,
and half-forgot the seasons, under that sky.

But time sprang from its coil and struck his heart,
and all the world shrank small as a grenade.
Over the sun of an idle afternoon
a doom of planes drew darkness like a shade.
Now, trapped in a mad traffic, he stands and sees

6

the map ruled off in squares of black and white,
and all his islands vanished with their palms
under the hostile despotism of night.

The Hawthorn Hedge

How long ago she planted the hawthorn hedge—
she forgets how long ago—
that barrier thorn across the hungry ridge;
thorn and snow.

It is twice as tall as the rider on the tall mare
who draws his reins to peer
in through the bee-hung blossom. Let him stare.
No one is here:

Only the mad old girl from the hut on the hill,
unkempt as an old tree.
She will hide away if you wave your hand or call;
she will not see.

Year-long, wind turns her grindstone heart and whets
a thornbranch like a knife,
shouting in winter "Death"; and when the white bud sets,
more loudly, "Life".

She has forgotten when she planted the hawthorn hedge,
that thorn, that green, that snow;
birdsong and sun dazzled across the ridge—
it was long ago.

Her hands were strong in the earth, her glance on the sky,
her song was sweet on the wind.
The hawthorn hedge took root, grew wild and high
to hide behind.

Nigger's Leap: New England

The eastward spurs tip backward from the sun.
Night runs an obscure tide round cape and bay
and beats with boats of cloud up from the sea
against this sheer and limelit granite head.
Swallow the spine of range; be dark, O lonely air.
Make a cold quilt across the bone and skull
that screamed falling in flesh from the lipped cliff
and then were silent, waiting for the flies.

Here is the symbol, and the climbing dark
a time for synthesis. Night buoys no warning
over the rocks that wait our keels; no bells
sound for her mariners. Now must we measure
our days by nights, our tropics by their poles,
love by its end and all our speech by silence.
See, in these gulfs, how small the light of home.

Did we not know their blood channelled our rivers,
and the black dust our crops ate was their dust?
O all men are one man at last. We should have known
the night that tided up the cliffs and hid them
had the same question on its tongue for us.
And there they lie that were ourselves writ small.

Never from earth again the coolamon,
or thin black children dancing like the shadows
of saplings in the wind. Night lips the harsh
scarp of the tableland and cools its granite.
Night floods us suddenly as history,
that has sunk many islands in its good time.

Bullocky

Beside his heavy-shouldered team,
thirsty with drought and chilled with rain,
he weathered all the striding years
till they ran widdershins in his brain:

Till the long solitary tracks
etched deeper with each lurching load
were populous before his eyes,
and fiends and angels used his road.

All the long straining journey grew
a mad apocalyptic dream,
and he old Moses, and the slaves
his suffering and stubborn team.

Then in his evening camp beneath
the half-light pillars of the trees
he filled the steepled cone of night
with shouted prayers and prophecies.

While past the campfire's crimson ring
the star-struck darkness cupped him round,
and centuries of cattle-bells
rang with their sweet uneasy sound.

Grass is across the wagon-tracks,
and plough strikes bone across the grass,
and vineyards cover all the slopes
where the dead teams were used to pass.

O vine, grow close upon that bone
and hold it with your rooted hand.
The prophet Moses feeds the grape,
and fruitful is the Promised Land.

Brother and Sisters

The road turned out to be a cul-de-sac;
stopped like a lost intention at the gate
and never crossed the mountains to the coast.
But they stayed on. Years grew like grass and leaves
across the half-erased and dubious track,
until one day they knew the plans were lost,
the blue-print for the bridge was out of date,
and now their orchards never would be planted.
The saplings sprouted slyly; day by day
the bush moved one step nearer, wondering when.
The polished parlour grew distrait and haunted
where Millie, Lucy, John each night at ten
wound the gilt clock that leaked the year away.

The pianola—oh, listen to the mocking-bird—
wavers on Sundays and has lost a note.
The wrinkled ewes snatch pansies through the fence
and stare with shallow eyes into the garden
where Lucy shrivels waiting for a word,
and Millie's cameos loosen round her throat.
The bush comes near, the ranges grow immense.

Feeding the lambs deserted in early spring
Lucy looked up and saw the stockman's eye
telling her she was cracked and old.
                                    The wall
groans in the night and settles more awry.
O how they lie awake. Their thoughts go fluttering
from room to room like moths: "Millie, are you asleep?"
"Oh John, I have been dreaming." "Lucy, do you cry?"
—meet tentative as moths. Antennae stroke a wing.
"There is nothing to be afraid of. Nothing at all."

South of My Days

South of my days' circle, part of my blood's country,
rises that tableland, high delicate outline
of bony slopes wincing under the winter;
low trees blue-leaved and olive; outcropping granite—
clean, lean, hungry country. The creek's leaf-silenced,
willow-choked, the slope a tangle of medlar and crab-apple,
branching over and under, blotched with a green lichen;
and the old cottage lurches in for shelter.

O cold the black-frost night. The walls draw in to the warmth
and the old roof cracks its joints; the slung kettle
hisses a leak on the fire. Hardly to be believed that summer
will turn up again some day in a wave of rambler roses,
thrust its hot face in here to tell another yarn—
a story old Dan can spin into a blanket against the winter.
Seventy years of stories he clutches round his bones.
Seventy summers are hived in him like old honey.

Droving that year, Charleville to the Hunter,
nineteen-one it was, and the drought beginning;
sixty head left at the McIntyre, the mud round them
hardened like iron; and the yellow boy died
in the sulky ahead with the gear, but the horse went on,
stopped at the Sandy Camp and waited in the evening.
It was the flies we seen first, swarming like bees.
Came to the Hunter, three hundred head of a thousand—
cruel to keep them alive—and the river was dust.

Or mustering up in the Bogongs in the autumn
when the blizzards came early. Brought them down; we
    brought them
down, what aren't there yet. Or driving for Cobb's on the run
up from Tamworth—Thunderbolt at the top of Hungry Hill,
and I give him a wink. I wouldn't wait long, Fred,
not if I was you; the troopers are just behind,

11

coming for that job at the Hillgrove. He went like a luny,
him on his big black horse.

                        Oh, they slide and they vanish
as he shuffles the years like a pack of conjuror's cards.
True or not, it's all the same; and the frost on the roof
cracks like a whip, and the back-log breaks into ash.
Wake, old man. This is winter, and the yarns are over.
No one is listening.
                  South of my days' circle
I know it dark against the stars, the high lean country
full of old stories that still go walking in my sleep.

The Surfer

He thrust his joy against the weight of the sea,
climbed through, slid under those long banks of foam—
(hawthorn hedges in spring, thorns in the face stinging).
How his brown strength drove through the hollow and coil
of green-through weirs of water!
Muscle of arm thrust down long muscle of water.
And swimming so, went out of sight
where mortal, masterful, frail, the gulls went wheeling
in air, as he in water, with delight.

Turn home, the sun goes down; swimmer, turn home.
Last leaf of gold vanishes from the sea-curve.
Take the big roller's shoulder, speed and swerve.
Come to the long beach home like a gull diving.

For on the sand the grey-wolf sea lies snarling;
cold twilight wind splits the waves' hair and shows
the bones they worry in their wolf-teeth. O, wind blows,
and sea crouches on sand, fawning and mouthing;
drops there and snatches again, drops and again snatches
its broken toys, its whitened pebbles and shells.

For New England

Your trees, the homesick and the swarthy native,
blow all one way to me, this southern weather
that smells of early snow. And I remember
the house closed in with sycamore and chestnut
fighting the foreign wind.
Here I will stay, she said; be done with the black north,
the harsh horizon rimmed with drought—
planted the island there and drew it round her.
Therefore I find in me the double tree.

And therefore I, deserted on the wharves,
have watched the ships fan out their web of streamers
(thinking of how the lookout at the Heads
leaned out towards the dubious rims of sea
to find a sail blown over like a message:
you are not forgotten);
or followed through the tap-root of the poplar. . .
But look, oh look, the Gothic tree's on fire
with blown galahs, and fuming with wild wings.

The hard inquiring wind strikes to the bone
and whines division. Many roads meet here
in me, the traveller and the ways I travel.
All the hills' gathered waters feed my seas
who am the swimmer and the mountain river;
and the long slopes' concurrence is my flesh
who am the gazer and the land I stare on;
and dogwood blooms within my winter blood,
and orchards fruit in me and need no season.
But sullenly the jealous bones recall
what other earth is shaped and hoarded in them.

Where's home, Ulysses? Cuckolded by lewd time
he never found again the girl he sailed from,
but at his fireside met the islands waiting,
and died there, twice a stranger.

                              Wind, blow through me,
till the nostalgic candles of laburnum
fuse with the dogwood in a single flame
to touch alight these sapless memories.
Then will my land turn sweetly from the plough
and all my pastures rise as green as spring.

The Moving Image

I

Here is the same clock that walked quietly
through those enormous years I half recall,
when between one blue summer and another
time seemed as many miles as round the world,
and world a day, a moment or a mile,
or a sweet slope of grass edged with the sea,
or a new song to sing, or a tree dressed in gold—
time and the world that faster spin, until
mind cannot grasp them now or heart take hold.

Only the sound of the clock is still the same.
Each of us followed it to a different hour
that like a bushranger held its guns on us
and forced our choice. And the clock begins to race.
We are caught in the endless circle of time and star
that never chime with the blood; we weary, we grow lame,
stumbling after their incessant pace
that slackens for us only when we are
caught deep in sleep, or music, or a lover's face.

Here where I walk was the green world of a child;
the infinity of day that closed in day,
the widening spiral turning and returning,
the same and not the same, that had no end.
Does the heart know no better than to pray

14

that time unwind its coil, the bone unbuild
till that lost world sit like a fruit in the hand—
till the felled trees rise upright where they lay
and leaves and birds spring on them as they stand?

And yet, the lovelier distance is ahead.
I would go farther with you, clock and star,
though the earth break under my feet and storm
snatch at my breath and night ride over me.
I am the maker. I have made both time and fear,
knowing that to yield to either is to be dead.
All that is real is to live, to desire, to be,
till I say to the child I was, "It is this; it is here.
In the doomed cell I have found love's whole eternity."

II

Dust blows harsh from the airfield; dust in the mouth.
This is the field that once was the world's end
(nothing beyond but hills water-hyacinth-coloured,
nothing in the field but supplejack and black-sally).
Dust blows back from the airfield; dust on the hand,
dust in the eyes that watch the plane turn north;
and to the plane the hills, the mysterious valley,
are bald and meagre as a map made out of sand—
hills of the wild horses, gullies of the rock-lily.

Looking from so high the world is evil and small
like a dried head from the islands with a grin of shell,
brittle and easy to break. But there is no end to the
    breaking—
one smashed, another mocks from your enemy's eye—
put that out, there's a world in every skull.
Nothing left but to pray, God save us all;
nothing but the tick of the clock and a world sucked dry;
nothing—till the tide of time come back to the full
and drown a man too sane, who climbed too high.

Till the tide of life come back, till time's great tide
roar from our depths and send us mad again
with a singing madness, like poor Tom of Bedlam—
poor Tom, through whose feverish blood life poured like
    thunder
till the frail floodgates burst within his brain,
and sleepless in his cell he sang and cried;
till the straw of his prison broke into flowers of wonder;
till the universe was the limit of his chain,
and galaxies glowed through the low roof he lay under.

All the lives that met in him and made
the tiny world of his life, his passion and skill,
shone for his eyes each as a separate star.
Age upon age of effort and terror and thought
stretched from his birth back to a single cell;
life upon life leapt from the fountaining seed,
lusted and took, hated, delighted and fought,
built from the thread of its dream a heaven and hell,
took up the search of man and died as it sought.

The first birth and the first cry and the first death,
the world of the first cell and the first man,
every sound and motion forgotten, remembered,
left their trace in his body, their voice in his speech.
One word in his mouth spread open like a fan,
the sound of it dwarfed the stars and stole his breath
as a million voices shouted it each to each;
and through the web of all their lives he ran
to grasp a glory never in one man's reach.

Poor Tom, in whose blood's intricate channelled track,
in the unsailed sea of his heart, in his witchball eyes,
in his senses that spoke and mind that shaped a world,
passionate terrible love never ceased burning;
who played with comets and stars like golden flies;
whose nights and days were whipmarks on his back;
whose birth and death were the sun and moon returning.
What songs shall a madman sing before he dies,
who makes one word of the song all life is learning?

Over the airfield looms the idol of night.
In its shadow the earth is spun by a stellar wind
in an eddy of spiralled stars. We are dwarfed by the dark.
We inherit a handful of dust and a fragment of stone.
Yet listen, the music grows; around us, before us, behind,
there is sound in the silence; the dark is a tremor of light.
It is the grass rising when winter is done.
It is the madmen singing, the lovers, the blind;
the cry of Tom of Bedlam, naked under the sun.

FROM
WOMAN TO MAN

Woman to Man

The eyeless labourer in the night,
the selfless, shapeless seed I hold,
builds for its resurrection day—
silent and swift and deep from sight
foresees the unimagined light.

This is no child with a child's face;
this has no name to name it by;
yet you and I have known it well.
This is our hunter and our chase,
the third who lay in our embrace.

This is the strength that your arm knows,
the arc of flesh that is my breast,
the precise crystals of our eyes.
This is the blood's wild tree that grows
the intricate and folded rose.

This is the maker and the made;
this is the question and reply;
the blind head butting at the dark,
the blaze of light along the blade.
Oh hold me, for I am afraid.

Woman's Song

O move in me, my darling,
for now the sun must rise;
the sun that will draw open
the lids upon your eyes.

O wake in me, my darling.
The knife of day is bright

to cut the thread that binds you
within the flesh of night.

Today I lose and find you
whom yet my blood would keep—
would weave and sing around you
the spells and songs of sleep.

None but I shall know you
as none but I have known;
yet there's a death and a maiden
who wait for you alone;

so move in me, my darling,
whose debt I cannot pay.
Pain and the dark must claim you,
and passion and the day.

Woman to Child

You who were darkness warmed my flesh
where out of darkness rose the seed.
Then all a world I made in me:
all the world you hear and see
hung upon my dreaming blood.

There moved the multitudinous stars,
and coloured birds and fishes moved.
There swam the sliding continents.
All time lay rolled in me, and sense,
and love that knew not its beloved.

O node and focus of the world—
I hold you deep within that well
you shall escape and not escape—

that mirrors still your sleeping shape,
that nurtures still your crescent cell.

I wither and you break from me;
yet though you dance in living light,
I am the earth, I am the root,
I am the stem that fed the fruit,
the link that joins you to the night.

Conch-shell

Virgin and clean the house is washed, and empty
the wave withdrawing leaves it to my hand.
The spiral passage turns upon itself.
The sweet enclosing curve of pearl
shuts in the room that was the cell of birth,
and is a windless shelter housing nothing.

Delicate argument and hieroglyph
of flesh that followed outward from the germ,
your line resolves the force that set its strength
against the wave's weight and the storm;
maps on my hand the puzzle, the perfection,
the brilliant arch from darkness into darkness.

And here, half-guess, half-knowledge, I contract
into a beast's blind orbit, stare deep down
the cliffs not I have climbed; your prodigal,
probe with my sense your senseless life—
since life, the force that leapt between your poles,
burns forward still in me against the night.

The Maker

I hold the crimson fruit
and plumage of the palm;
flame-tree, that scarlet spirit,
in my soil takes root.

My days burn with the sun,
my nights with moon and star,
since into myself I took
all living things that are.

All things that glow and move,
all things that change and pass,
I gather their delight
as in a burning-glass;

all things I focus in
the crystal of my sense.
I give them breath and life
and set them free in the dance.

I am a tranquil lake
to mirror their joy and pain;
and all their pain and joy
I from my own heart make,

since love, who cancels fear
with his fixed will,
burned my vision clear
and bid my sense be still.

The Sisters

In the vine-shadows on the veranda,
under the yellow leaves, in the cooling sun,
sit the two sisters. Their slow voices run
like little winter creeks dwindled by frost and wind,
and the square of sunlight moves on the veranda.

They remember the gay young men on their tall horses
who came courting; the dancing and the smells of leather
and wine; the girls whispering by the fire together;
even their dolls and ponies—all they have left behind
moves in the yellow shadows on the veranda.

Thinking of their lives apart and the men they married,
thinking of the marriage-bed and the birth of the first child,
they look down smiling. "My life was wide and wild,
and who can know my heart? There in that golden jungle
I walk alone," say the old sisters on the veranda.

Spring After War

Winter and spring the clouds drift in,
and mist is grey as moving sheep
where ewe goes heavy in lamb, and ewe
beside her lamb lies half-asleep,
her narrow sides with milk drawn thin.

How reconcile the alien eyes,
the warring life how reconcile?
On the lean slope and dripping hill
the sheep move slowly, single-file.
Where is it the heart's country lies?

The rope-vines hang where the clouds move.
The scorpion dances in the brain.
The years of death rattle their bones.
The ewe cries in the pitiless rain
the mortal cry of anguished love.

Which is the country, which is true?
How reconcile the treacherous earth,
the gaping flesh how reconcile—
and still move forward to some birth,
as the lamb moves within the ewe?

Within the bones the scorpion lay.
Within the bones the lamb was made.
Within the bones the heart is housed.
The blood that leaps behind the blade
is death or life; is night or day.

The knife goes back into its sheath;
the lamb comes struggling from the womb;
the seeking flesh has found its goal.
The compass heart swings seeking home
between the lands of life and death.

Camphor Laurel

Here in the slack of night
the tree breathes honey and moonlight.
Here in the blackened yard
smoke and time and use have marred,
leaning from that fantan gloom
the bent tree is heavy in bloom.

The dark house creaks and sways;
"Not like the old days."
Tim and Sam and ragbag Nell,

Wong who keeps the Chinese hell,
the half-caste lovers, the humpbacked boy,
sleep for sorrow or wake for joy.

Under the house the roots go deep,
down, down, while the sleepers sleep;
splitting the rock where the house is set,
cracking the paved and broken street.
Old Tim turns and old Sam groans,
"God be good to my breaking bones";
and in the slack of tideless night
the tree breathes honey and moonlight.

The Garden

Flowers of red silk and purple velvet grew
under the humming may-tree; the huge pines
made night across the grass, where the black snake
went whispering in its coils; and moving sunlight drew
copper fingers through the apple-trees.
Warm is the light the summer day refines;

and warm is she, whom life has made secure.
Walking slow along her garden ways,
a bee grown old at summer's end, she dips
and drinks that honey. All that we endure,
all that we meet and live through, gathers in our old age
and makes a shelter from the cold, she says.

Pulling around her shoulders her Joseph's-coat,
small bright bouquets reflected in her eyes,
this is the night's fit enemy and good friend
who has felt often his black hand at her throat;
and therefore my heart chose her, scarecrow, bag of old
    bones,
Eve walking with her snake and butterfly.

The World and the Child

I

This is the child. He has not yet put out leaves.
His bare skin tastes the air; his naked eyes
know nothing but strange shapes. Nothing is named;
nothing is ago, nothing not yet. Death is that which dies,
and goes no farther; for the mere dead he grieves,
and grief has yet no meaning and no size.

Where the wild harebell grows to a blue cave
and the climbing ant is a monster of green light
the child clings to his grassblade. The mountain range
lies like a pillow for his head at night,
the moon swings from his ceiling. He is a wave
that timeless moves through time, imperishably bright.

Yet what is it that moves? What is the unresting hunger
that shapes the soft-fleshed face, makes the bones harden?
Rebel—rebel, it cries. Never be satisfied.
Do not weaken for their grief; do not give in or pardon.
Only through this pain, this black desire, this anger,
shall you at last return to your lost garden.

II

Out of himself like a thread the child spins pain
and makes a net to catch the unknown world.
Words gather there heavy as fish, and tears,
and tales of love and of the polar cold.
Now, says the child, I shall never be young again.
The shadow of my net has darkened the sea's gold.

Yet what is it that draws the net and throws?
Forget to be young, it says: forget to be afraid.
No net is strong enough to hold the world,
nor man of such a sinew ever was made.

What is the world? That secret no man knows;
yet look, beyond the sundazzle, the blinding blade—
was not that the white waterfall from some vast side?

Nets have been breached and men have died in vain.
No net is strong enough to hold the world.
Yet gather in your bleeding hands your net again—
not till Leviathan's beached shall you be satisfied.

Night After Bushfire

There is no more silence on the plains of the moon,
and time is no more alien there, than here.
Sun thrust his warm hand down at the high noon,
but all that stirred was the faint dust of fear.

Charred death upon the rock leans his charred bone
and stares at death from sockets black with flame.
Man, if he come to brave that glance alone,
must leave behind his human home and name.

Carry like a threatened thing your soul away,
and do not look too long to left or right,
for he whose soul wears the strict chains of day
will lose it in this landscape of charcoal and moonlight.

The Bull

In the olive darkness of the sally-trees
silently moved the air from night to day.
The summer-grass was thick with honey-daisies
where he, a curled god, a red Jupiter,
heavy with power among his women lay.

But summer's bubble-sound of sweet creek-water
dwindles and is silent; the seeding grasses
grow harsh, and wind and frost in the black sallies
roughen the sleek-haired slopes. Seek him out, then,
the angry god betrayed, whose godhead passes,

and down the hillsides drive him from his mob.
What enemy steals his strength—what rival steals
his mastered cows? His thunders powerless,
the red storm of his body shrunk with fear,
runs the great bull, the dogs upon his heels.

The Cycads

Their smooth dark flames flicker at time's own root.
Round them the rising forests of the years
alter the climates of forgotten earth
and silt with leaves the strata of first birth.

Only the antique cycads sullenly
keep the old bargain life has long since broken;
and, cursed by age, through each chill century
they watch the shrunken moon, but never die,

for time forgets the promise he once made,
and change forgets that they are left alone.
Among the complicated birds and flowers
they seem a generation carved in stone.

Leaning together, down those gulfs they stare
over whose darkness dance the brilliant birds
that cry in air one moment, and are gone;
and with their countless suns the years spin on.

Take their cold seed and set it in the mind,
and its slow root will lengthen deep and deep

till, following, you cling on the last ledge
over the unthinkable, unfathomed edge
beyond which man remembers only sleep.

The Twins

Not because of their beauty—though they are slender
as saplings of white cedar, and long as lilies—
not because of their delicate dancing step,
or their brown hair sideways blown like the manes of fillies—
it is not for their beauty that the crowd in the street
wavers like dry leaves around them on the wind.
It is the chord, the intricate unison
of one and one, strikes home to the watcher's mind.

How sweet is the double gesture, the mirror-answer;
same hand woven in same, like arm in arm.
Salt blood like tears freshens the crowd's dry veins,
and moving in its web of time and harm
the unloved heart asks, "Where is my reply,
my kin, my answer? I am driven and alone."
Their serene eyes seek nothing. They walk by.
They move into the future and are gone.

Eli, Eli

To see them go by drowning in the river—
Soldiers and elders drowning in the river,
the pitiful women drowning in the river,
the children's faces staring from the river—
that was his cross, and not the cross they gave him.

To hold the invisible wand, and not to save them—
to know them turned to death, and yet not save them;
only to cry to them and not to save them,
knowing that no one but themselves could save them—
this was the wound, more than the wound they dealt him.

To hold out love and know they would not take it,
to hold out faith and know they dared not take it—
the invisible wand, and none would see or take it;
all he could give, and there was none to take it—
thus they betrayed him, not with the tongue's betrayal.

He watched, and they were drowning in the river;
faces like sodden flowers in the river,
faces of children moving in the river;
and all the while, he knew there was no river.

The Unborn

I

I know no sleep you do not stand beside.
You footless darkness following where I go,
you lipless drinker at my drowsy breast—
yet whom I must deny I have denied.
The unpossessing is the unpossessed.

Slight is the foothold from the well of night;
the stair is broken and the keys are lost,
and you whom I have wrecked are wrecked indeed;
and yet you stand upon the edge of sight
and I have known no path you have not crossed.

The shadow wakeful on my sleeping arm
stares from the hidden depths far under birth.
How like a diamond looks the far-off day,

that crystal that reflects your darkened dream,
that bubble of sunlight broken and blown away.
O gift ungiven. O uncreated earth.

II

Not even tears were mine,
not even death;
not even the dazzling pain
of one first breath.

I never knew the sleep
of the warm womb.
The end of my beginning
was dumb; was dumb.

Only the foot of the stair
I felt, being blind.
Then came the touch of fear
time now can never mend.

My name was a dark sound
that made no word.
Terror alone spoke it
and nothing heard.

Neither awake nor asleep,
on the rack of dark I lie,
hearing my own not-voice:
"What was I? I? I?"

Night

Standing here in the night
we are turned to a great tree,
every leaf a star,
its root eternity.

So deeply goes its root
into the world's womb,
so high rises its stem,
it leaves for death no room.

We are turned to a great tree
hung with heavy fruit,
torn by the winds of time
and the worm at the root.

Come back to the kind flesh,
to love and simple sight.
Let us forget awhile
that we create the night.

Out of this dark of time,
alive and human, come.
Brief is the warm day
wherein we have our home.

The Killer

The day was clear as fire,
the birds sang frail as glass,
when thirsty I came to the creek
and fell by its side in the grass.

My breast on the bright moss
and shower-embroidered weeds,
my lips to the live water
I saw him turn in the reeds.

Black horror sprang from the dark
in a violent birth,
and through its cloth of grass
I felt the clutch of earth.

O beat him into the ground.
O strike him till he dies—
or else your life itself
drains through those colourless eyes.

I struck again and again.
Slender in black and red
he lies, and his icy glance
turns outward, clear and dead.

But nimble my enemy
as water is, or wind.
He has slipped from his death aside
and vanished into my mind.

He has vanished whence he came,
my nimble enemy;
and the ants come out to the snake
and drink at his shallow eye.

Metho Drinker

Under the death of winter's leaves he lies
who cried to Nothing and the terrible night
to be his home and bread. "O take from me
the weight and waterfall of ceaseless Time
that batters down my weakness; the knives of light
whose thrust I cannot turn; the cruelty
of human eyes that dare not touch nor pity."
Under the worn leaves of the winter city
safe in the house of Nothing now he lies.

His white and burning girl, his woman of fire,
creeps to his heart and sets a candle there
to melt away the flesh that hides the bone,
to eat the nerve that tethers him in Time.

He will lie warm until the bone is bare
and on a dead dark moon he wakes alone.
It was for Death he took her; death is but this;
and yet he is uneasy under her kiss
and winces from that acid of her desire.

The Old Prison

The rows of cells are unroofed,
a flute for the wind's mouth,
who comes with a breath of ice
from the blue caves of the south.

O dark and fierce day:
the wind like an angry bee
hunts for the black honey
in the pits of the hollow sea.

Waves of shadow wash
the empty shell bone-bare,
and like a bone it sings
a bitter song of air.

Who built and laboured here?
The wind and the sea say
—Their cold nest is broken
and they are blown away.

They did not breed nor love.
Each in his cell alone
cried as the wind now cries
through this flute of stone.

Midnight

Darkness where I find my sight,
shadowless and burning night,
here where death and life are met
is the fire of being set.

Watchman eye and workman hand
are spun of water, air and sand.
These will crumble and be gone—
still that darkness rages on.

As a plant in winter dies
down into the germ, and lies
leafless, tongueless, lost in earth,
imaging its fierce rebirth;

and with the whirling rays of the sun
and shuttle-stroke of living rain
weaves that image from its heart
and like a god is born again—

so let my blood reshape its dream,
drawn into that tideless stream;
that shadowless and burning night
of darkness where I find my sight.

Wonga Vine

Look down; be still.
The sunburst day's on fire,
O twilight bell,
flower of the wonga vine.

I gather you
out of his withering light.
Sleep there, red;
sleep there, yellow and white.

Move as the creek
moves to its hidden pool.
The sun has eyes of fire;
be my white waterfall.

Lie on my eyes like hands,
let no sun shine—
O twilight bell,
flower of the wonga vine.

Flame-tree in a Quarry

From the broken bone of the hill,
stripped and left for dead,
like a wrecked skull
leaps out this bush of blood.

Out of the torn earth's mouth
comes the old cry of praise.
Still is the song made flesh
though the singer dies—

flesh of the world's delight,
voice of the world's desire,
I drink you with my sight
and I am filled with fire.

Out of the very wound
springs up this scarlet breath—
this fountain of hot joy,
this living ghost of death.

The Blind Man

I *The Dust in the Township*

Under the Moreton Bay fig by the war memorial
blind Jimmy Delaney sits alone and sings
in the pollen-coloured dust; and Jimmy Delaney,
coloured like the dust, is of that dust
three generations made. Sing for the dust
then, Jimmy, thin and strange as old fiddle-strings
or the dry wires of grass-stems stretched in the thrust
of a winter westerly; and if it's true
black Mary's your father's mother, none better than you
can speak in the voice of the forgotten dust.

Horrie Delaney came here first with cattle,
and shook the dust out of its golden sleep—
the golden sleep of eternal generation.
Grass, wattle and messmate-tree and earth:
death bearing life, and both come out of earth.
Deeper than the shadows of trees and tribes, deep
lay the spring that issues in death and birth.
Horrie Delaney with his dogs and his gun
came like another shadow between the earth and the sun
and now with the tribes he is gone down in death.

Dick Delaney the combo cleared these hills.
Easily the bush fell and lightly, now it seems
to us who forget the sweat of Dick Delaney,
and the humpy and the scalding sunlight and the black
hate between the white skin and the black.
The smoke sang upward, the trees vanished like dreams
and the long hills lie naked as a whipped back.
Greed and hunger tear at the marrow-bone,
and the heart in the breast hangs heavy as a great gold stone.
Under the marred earth, his bones twist on that rack.

Yellow Delaney is the third of that name,
and like the yellow dust, he finds no rest.
Landless and loveless, he went wandering
with his despised white girl, and left no track
but the black mark of a campfire. How can they die
who live without a country? He does not die
though like the night curlew the blood mourns in his breast
and gets no answer. Under the tenantless sky
he lives by his traps in the lost ranges; he
is the brain-fever bird calling from a rung tree
that time is a cracked mask and day a golden lie.

Under the Moreton Bay fig by the war memorial
Jimmy Delaney the blind man sits and sings
where the wind raises dry fountains of faded gold.
No one has loved or sung of the unregarded dust.
Dance upright in the wind, dry-voiced and humble dust,
out of whose breast the great green fig-tree springs,
and the proud man, and the singer, and the outcast.
All are but shadows between the earth and the sun,
sings Jimmy Delaney, sitting where the dust-whirls run,
columns of dancing dust that sink at last.

And yet those men, this fallen dust, these shadows
remembered only by the blind man whose songs none hear,
sting him in the noon sunlight as a hornet stings.
The conqueror who possessed a world alone,
and he who hammered a world on his heart's stone,
and last the man whose world splintered in fear—
their shadows lengthen in the light of noon,
their dust bites deep, driven by a restless wind.
O singer, son of darkness, love that is blind,
sing for the golden dust that dances and is gone.

II *Country Dance*

The dance in the township hall is nearly over.
Hours ago the stiff-handed wood-cheeked women
got up from the benches round the walls

and took home their aching eyes and weary children.
Mrs McLarty with twenty cows to milk
before dawn, went with the music stinging
like sixty wasps under her best dress.
Eva Callaghan whose boy died in the army
sat under the streamers like a house to let
and went alone, a black pot brimming with tears.
"Once my body was a white cedar, my breasts the buds on
    the quince-tree,
that now are fallen and grey like logs on a cleared hill.
Then why is my blood not quiet? what is the good
of the whips of music stinging along my blood?"

The dance in the township hall is nearly over.
Outside in the yard the fire like a great red city
eats back into the log, its noisy flames fallen.
Jimmy Dunn has forgotten his camp in the hills,
and sleeps like a heap of rags beside a bottle.
The young boys sit and stare at the heart of the city
thinking of the neon lights and the girls at the corners
with lips like coals and thighs as silver as florins.
Jock Hamilton thinks of the bally cow gone sick
and the cockatoos in the corn and the corn ready to pick,
and the wires in the thirty-acre broken.
Oh, what rats nibble at the cords of our nerves?
When will the wires break, the ploughed paddocks lie open,
the bow of the fiddle saw through the breastbone,
the dream be done, and we waken?

Streamers and boughs are falling, the dance grows faster.
Only the lovers and the young are dancing
now at the end of the dance, in a trance or singing.
Say the lovers locked together and crowned with coloured
    paper:
"The bit of black glass I picked up out of the campfire
is the light that the moon puts on your hair."
"The green pool I swam in under the willows
is the drowning depth, the summer night of your eyes."
"You are the death I move to." "O burning weapon,
you are the pain I long for."

Stars, leaves and streamers fall in the dark dust
and the blind man lies alone in his sphere of night.

Oh, I
red centre of a dark and burning sky,
fit my words to music, my crippled words to music,
and sing to the fire with the voice of the fire.
Go sleep with your grief, go sleep with your desire,
go deep into the core of night and silence.
But I hold all of it, your hate and sorrow,
your passion and your fear; I am the breath
that holds you from your death.
I am the voice of music and the ended dance.

III *Lost Child*

Is the boy lost? Then I know where he is gone.
He has gone climbing the terrible crags of the sun.

The searchers go through the green valley, shouting his
    name;
the dogs are moaning on the hill for the scent of his track;
but the men will all be hoarse and the dogs lame
before the Hamiltons' boy is found or comes back.
Through the smouldering ice of the moon he is stumbling
    alone.
I shall rise from my dark and follow where he is gone.

I heard from my bed his bugle breath go by
and the drum of his heart in the measure of an old song.
I shall travel into silence, and in that fierce country
when we meet he will know he has been away too long.
They are looking for him now in the vine-scrub over the hill,
but I think he is alone in a place that I know well.

Is the boy lost? Then I know where he is gone.
He is climbing to Paradise up a river of stars and stone.

IV *Blind Man's Song*

No one but a child or a fool dares
to listen to silence, or to the words of my song.
Silence goes back into the man who hears
and carries all the sorrow was ever in his ears
and all the fear he has gathered all his life long;
and this song is a fool's song.

The old man and the young man saw me lie
like a yellow snake in the dust when the dust was still.
The whispering song of the wind or the snake sang I,
and the old man turned his head away and went by,
and the young man set his horse full speed at the hill;
but the song went on still.

I have the tune of the singer who makes men afraid.
I repeat the small speech of the worm in the ground,
and out of the depths of the rock my words are made.
I have laid my ear to the dust, and the thing it said
was Silence. Therefore I have made silence speak; I found
for the night a sound.

So no one but a fool or a lonely child
will turn his head to listen to my song.
I am the yellow snake with a dark, a double tongue,
speaking from the dust to the two rulers of the world.

FROM
THE GATEWAY

Dark Gift

The flower begins in the dark
where life is not.
Death has a word to speak
and the flower begins.

How small, how closely bound
in nothing's net
the word waits in the ground
for the cloak earth spins.

The root goes down in the night
and from night's mud
the unmade, the inchoate,
starts to take shape and rise.

The blind, the upward hand
clenches its bud.
What message does death send
from the grave where he lies?

Open, green hand, and give
the dark gift you hold.

Oh wild mysterious gold!
Oh act of passionate love!

Fire at Murdering Hut

I *The Grave*

You who were the snake hidden under my house,
the breath of the bushfire—
are you come to take me again, like a storm in the night,

oh storm of my desire?
Are you come to take me like a knife in the breast
after this silent century?
You will find me this time lying alone.
It has been a long time you have left me with the rose-tree,
the wandering mist and the stone.

Lay down your fire beside my frost again,
against my stone your blade.
I have been too long alone in the drought and rain:
it is all true as you said.
Come now and take me—
dig with the blade of your heart into the grave and wake me,
and this time you will find me lying alone.
I have been here too long with the white rose-tree,
the wandering mist and the stone.

II *The Fire*

Are you one of the old dead, whisperer under my feet?
I stamp on your shallow earth
like a red bird; my song is the last message of love,
which is the news of death.
Now I shall eat even your white roses, and eat
the dry moss on your stone.
Neither love nor death come to the dead, nor does flesh
grow on the bared bone.

But look, I am beautiful, I dance on your grave
like a lover's ghost.
I dance with your tree of roses, I whirl my blade
till they fall into black dust.
And though I am not your lover and am not love,
I shall set before I am gone
a kiss on the rose-root to travel down to your breast:
the last message of love, the fire's black stain
to wear like a badge over your white breastbone.

III *The Stone*

Cruel was the steel in the hand that split my sleep
and branded me with pain.
Why did I not lie forever out of time's way,
cold, quiet and deep?
Now I am delivered to the fire again
and set naked in the track of merciless day
for the years to fret me, those instruments of love
that will eat my stone away.

You, the poor nakedness that lies beneath—
the bone that love left bare—
I hear you call on him, the terrible one,
the eater even of death.
If I were hidden in earth, I should lie quiet there
and forget the summoning cry of the wild sun,
and forget the fire that would crack open my breast
for love to tear.

Why can you not lie quiet as the knife
that rots beside your bone?
It is because the stuff that life has once possessed
is ever starved for life.
And that is why I am afraid of the stab of the sun
and the rain's hands beating my breast.
Fire, do not open my heart. I do not wish to wake
to the cruel day of love. Leave me my rest.

The Cedars

The dried body of winter is hard to kill.
Frost crumbles the dead bracken, greys the old grass,
and the great hemisphere of air goes flying
barren and cold from desert or polar seas,
tattering fern and leaf. By the sunken pool
the sullen Sodom-apple grips his scarlet fruit.

Spring, returner, knocker at the iron gates,
why should you return? None wish to live again.
Locked in our mourning, in our sluggish age,
we stand and think of past springs, of deceits not yet
    forgotten.
Then we answered you in youth and joy; we threw
open our strongholds, and hung our walls with flowers.
Do not ask us to answer again as then we answered.

For it is anguish to be reborn and reborn:
at every return of the overmastering season
to shed our lives in pain, to waken into the cold,
to become naked, while with unbearable effort
we make way for the new sap that burns along old
    channels—
while out of our life's substance, the inmost of our being,
form those brief flowers, those sacrifices, soon falling,
which spring the returner demands, and demands for ever.

Easier, far easier, to stand with downturned eyes
and hands hanging, to let age and mourning cover us
with their dark rest, heavy like death, like the ground
from which we issued and towards which we crumble.
Easier to be one with the impotent body of winter,
and let our old leaves rattle on the wind's currents—
to stand like the rung trees whose boughs no longer murmur
their foolish answers to spring; whose blossoms now are
the only lasting flowers, the creeping lichens of death.

Spring, impatient, thunderer at the doors of iron,
we have no songs left. Let our boughs be silent.
Hold back your fires that would sear us into flower again,
and your insistent bees, the messengers of generation.
Our bodies are old as winter and would remain in winter.
So the old trees plead, clinging to the edge of darkness.

But round their roots the mintbush makes its buds ready
and the snake in hiding feels the sunlight's finger.
The snake, the fang of summer, beauty's double meaning,
shifts his slow coils and feels his springtime hunger.

Train Journey

Glassed with cold sleep and dazzled by the moon,
out of the confused hammering dark of the train
I looked and saw under the moon's cold sheet
your delicate dry breasts, country that built my heart;

and the small trees on their uncoloured slope
like poetry moved, articulate and sharp
and purposeful under the great dry flight of air,
under the crosswise currents of wind and star.

Clench down your strength, box-tree and ironbark.
Break with your violent root the virgin rock.
Draw from the flying dark its breath of dew
till the unliving come to life in you.

Be over the blind rock a skin of sense,
under the barren height a slender dance . . .

I woke and saw the dark small trees that burn
suddenly into flowers more lovely than the white moon.

Myth

A god has chosen to be shaped in flesh.
He has put on the garment of the world.
A blind and sucking fish, a huddled worm,
he crouches here until his time shall come,
all the dimensions of his glory furled
into the blood and clay of the night's womb.
Eternity is locked in time and form.

Within those mole-dark corridors of earth
how can his love be born and how unfold?

Eternal knowledge in an atom's span
is bound by its own strength with its own chain.
The nerve is dull, the eyes are stopped with mould,
the flesh is slave of accident or pain.
Sunk in his brittle prison-cell of mud,
the god who once chose to become a man
is now a man who must become a god.

Eroded Hills

These hills my father's father stripped;
and, beggars to the winter wind,
they crouch like shoulders naked and whipped—
humble, abandoned, out of mind.

Of their scant creeks I drank once
and ate sour cherries from old trees
found in their gullies fruiting by chance.
Neither fruit nor water gave my mind ease.

I dream of hills bandaged in snow,
their eyelids clenched to keep out fear.
When the last leaf and bird go
let my thoughts stand like trees here.

Old House

Where now outside the weary house the pepperina,
that great broken tree, gropes with its blind hands
and sings a moment in the magpie's voice, there he stood
    once,
that redhaired man my great-great-grandfather,
his long face amiable as an animal's,

and thought of vines and horses.
He moved in that mindless country like a red ant,
running tireless in the summer heat among the trees—
the nameless trees, the sleeping soil, the original river—
and said that the eastern slope would do for a vineyard.

In the camp by the river they made up songs about him,
songs about the wagons, songs about the cattle,
songs about the horses and the children and the woman.
These were a dream, something strayed out of a dream.
They would vanish down the river, but the river would flow
    on;
under the river-oaks the river would flow on;
winter and summer would burn the grass white
or red like the red of the pale man's hair.
In the camp by the river they made up those songs
and my great-great-grandfather heard them with one part of
    his mind.

And in those days
there was one of him and a thousand of them;
and in these days none are left—
neither a pale man with kangaroo-grass hair
nor a camp of dark singers mocking by the river.
And the trees and the creatures, all of them are gone.
But the sad river, the silted river,
under its dark banks the river flows on,
the wind still blows and the river still flows.
And the great broken tree, the dying pepperina,
clutches in its hands the fragments of a song.

Drought Year

That time of drought the embered air
burned to the roots of timber and grass.
The crackling lime-scrub would not bear

and Mooni Creek was sand that year.
The dingoes' cry was strange to hear.

I heard the dingoes cry
in the whipstick scrub on the Thirty-mile Dry.
I saw the wagtail take his fill
perching in the seething skull.
I saw the eel wither where he curled
in the last blood-drop of a spent world.

I heard the bone whisper in the hide
of the big red horse that lay where he died.
Prop that horse up, make him stand,
hoofs turned down in the bitter sand—
make him stand at the gate of the Thirty-mile Dry,
—Turn this way and you will die—
and strange and loud was the dingoes' cry.

Flood Year

Walking up the driftwood beach at day's end,
I saw it, thrust up out of a hillock of sand—
a frail bleached clench of fingers dried by wind—
the dead child's hand?

And they are mourning there still, though I forget,
the year of flood, the scoured ruined land,
the herds gone down the current, the farms drowned,
and the child never found.

When I was there the thick hurling waters
had gone back to the river; the farms were almost drained.
Banished half-dead cattle searched the dunes; it rained;
river and sea met with a wild sound.

Oh with a wild sound water flung into air
where sea met river; all the country round
no heart was quiet. I walked on the driftwood sand
and saw the pale crab crouched, and came to a stand,
thinking: A child's hand? The child's hand?

Birds

Whatever the bird is, is perfect in the bird.
Weapon kestrel hard as a blade's curve,
thrush round as a mother or a full drop of water,
fruit-green parrot wise in his shrieking swerve—
all are what bird is and do not reach beyond bird.

Whatever the bird does is right for the bird to do—
cruel kestrel dividing in his hunger the sky,
thrush in the trembling dew beginning to sing,
parrot clinging and quarrelling and veiling his queer eye—
all these are as birds are and good for birds to do.

But I am torn and beleaguered by my own people.
The blood that feeds my heart is the blood they gave me,
and my heart is the house where they gather and fight for
    dominion—
all different, all with a wish and a will to save me,
to turn me into the ways of other people.

If I could leave their battleground for the forest of a bird
I could melt the past, the present and the future in one
and find the words that lie behind all these languages.
Then I could fuse my passions into one clear stone
and be simple to myself as the bird is to the bird.

Lion

Lion, let your desert eyes
turn on me.
Look beyond my flesh and see
that in it which never dies;

that which neither sleeps nor wakes—
the pool of glass
where no wave rocks or breaks,
where no days or nights pass.

Your shining eyes like the sun will find
an image there
that will answer stare for stare
till with its gaze your eyes are blind.

Though you wear the face of the sun
in the mortal gold of your eyes,
yet till that Lord himself dies
this deeper image will live on.

It is the crystal glance of love
earth turns on sun as the two move;
it is the jewel I was given
in exchange for your heaven.

Phaius Orchid

Out of the brackish sand
see the phaius orchid build
her intricate moonlight tower
that rusts away in flower.

For whose eyes—for whose eyes
does this blind being weave
sand's poverty, water's sour,
the white and black of the hour

into the image I hold
and cannot understand?
Is it for the ants, the bees,
the lizard outside his cave,

or is it to garland time—
eternity's cold tool
that severs with its blade
the gift as soon as made?

Then I too am time's fool.
What can I do but believe?
Here like the plant I weave
your dying garlands, time.

Eden

This is the grief of the heart—
that it can never be
closed in one flesh with its love,
like the fruit hung on Eve's tree:

this the lament of the flesh—
that it must always contain
the uncompleted heart,
greedy of love and pain.

—This is not what I desired,
the flesh in anguish cries;
—the gift that was made to me
in my lost Paradise,

where in predestined joy
and with a shock like death
the two halves of my being
met to make one truth.

Yet where the circle was joined
the desperate chase began;
where love in love dissolved
sprang up the woman and man;

and locked in the pangs of life
sway those unwilling selves
till the circle join again
and love in love dissolves.

The Pool and the Star

Let me be most clear and most tender;
let no wind break my perfection.
Let the stream of my life run muted,
and a pure sleep unbar
my every depth and secret.

I wait for the rising of a star
whose spear of light shall transfix me—
of a far-off world whose silence
my very truth must answer.
That shaft shall pierce me through
till I cool its white-hot metal.

Let move no leaf nor moth;
sleep quietly, all my creatures.
I must be closed as the rose is
until that bright one rises.
Then down the fall of space
his kiss the shape of a star
shall wake the dark of my breast.

For this I am drawn from far—
for this I am gathered together.
Though made of time and of waters
that move even while I love,
I shall draw from the living day
no hour as pure, as bright,
as this when across the night
he stoops with his steady ray
and his image burns on my breast.

All Things Conspire

All things conspire to hold me from you—
even my love,
since that would mask you and unname you
till merely woman and man we live.
All men wear arms against the rebel;
and they are wise,
since the sound world they know and stable
is eaten away by lovers' eyes.

All things conspire to stand between us—
even you and I,
who still command us, still unjoin us,
and drive us forward till we die.
Not till those fiery ghosts are laid
shall we be one.
Till then, they whet our double blade
and use the turning world for stone.

The Flame-tree

How to live, I said, as the flame-tree lives?
To know what the flame-tree knows—to be
prodigal of my life as that wild tree
and wear my passion so?
That lover's knot of water and earth and sun,
that easy answer to the question baffling reason,
branches out of my heart, this sudden season.
I know what I would know.

How shall I thank you, who teach me how to wait
in quietness for the hour to ask or give:
to take and in taking bestow, in bestowing live:
in the loss of myself, to find?
This is the flame-tree; look how gloriously
that careless blossomer scatters, and more, and more.
What the earth takes of her, it will restore.
These are the thanks of lovers who share one mind.

Legend

The blacksmith's boy went out with a rifle
and a black dog running behind.
Cobwebs snatched at his feet,
rivers hindered him,
thorn-branches caught at his eyes to make him blind
and the sky turned into an unlucky opal,
but he didn't mind.
I can break branches, I can swim rivers, I can stare out any
    spider I meet,
said he to his dog and his rifle.

The blacksmith's boy went over the paddocks
with his old black hat on his head.

Mountains jumped in his way,
rocks rolled down on him,
and the old crow cried, You'll soon be dead;
and the rain came down like mattocks.
But he only said
I can climb mountains, I can dodge rocks, I can shoot an old
    crow any day.
And he went on over the paddocks.

When he came to the end of the day the sun began falling.
Up came the night ready to swallow him,
like the barrel of a gun,
like an old black hat,
like a black dog hungry to follow him.
Then the pigeon, the magpie and the dove began wailing,
and the grass lay down to pillow him.
His rifle broke, his hat blew away and his dog was gone,
and the sun was falling.

But in front of the night the rainbow stood on the mountain
just as his heart foretold.
He ran like a hare,
he climbed like a fox,
he caught it in his hands, the colours and the cold—
like a bar of ice, like the column of a fountain,
like a ring of gold.
The pigeon, the magpie and the dove flew up to stare,
and the grass stood up again on the mountain.

The blacksmith's boy hung the rainbow on his shoulder,
instead of his broken gun.
Lizards ran out to see,
snakes made way for him,
and the rainbow shone as brightly as the sun.
All the world said, Nobody is braver, nobody is bolder,
nobody else has done
anything to equal it. He went home as easy as could be
with the swinging rainbow on his shoulder.

The Cicadas

On yellow days in summer when the early heat
presses like hands hardening the sown earth
into stillness, when after sunrise birds fall quiet
and streams sink in their beds and in silence meet,
then underground the blind nymphs waken and move.
They must begin at last to struggle towards love.

For a whole life they have crouched alone and dumb,
in patient ugliness enduring the humble dark.
Nothing has shaken that world below the world
except the far-off thunder, the strain of roots in storm.
Sunk in an airless night they neither slept nor woke,
but hanging on the tree's blood dreamed vaguely the dreams
    of the tree,
and put on wavering leaves, wing-veined, too delicate to see.

But now in terror overhead their day of dying breaks.
The trumpet of the rising sun bursts into sound
and the implacable unborn stir and reply.
In the hard shell an unmade body wakes
and fights to break from its motherly-enclosing ground.
These dead must dig their upward grave in fear
to cast the living into the naked air.

Terrible is the pressure of light into the heart.
The womb is withered and cracked, the birth is begun,
and shuddering and groaning to break that iron grasp
the new is delivered as the old is torn apart.
Love whose unmerciful blade has pierced us through,
we struggle naked from our death in search of you.

This is the wild light that our dreams foretold
while unaware we prepared these eyes and wings—
while in our sleep we learned the song the world sings.
Sing now, my brothers; climb to that intolerable gold.

Full Moon Rhyme

There's a hare in the moon tonight,
crouching alone in the bright
buttercup field of the moon;
and all the dogs in the world
howl at the hare in the moon.

"I chased that hare to the sky,"
the hungry dogs all cry.
"The hare jumped into the moon
and left me here in the cold.
I chased that hare to the moon."

"Come down again, wild hare.
We can see you there,"
the dogs all howl to the moon.
"Come down again to the world,
you mad black hare in the moon,

"or we will grow wings and fly
up to the star-grassed sky
to hunt you out of the moon,"
the hungry dogs of the world
howl at the hare in the moon.

To a Child

When I was a child I saw
a burning bird in a tree.
I see became *I am*,
I am became *I see*.

In winter dawns of frost
the lamp swung in my hand.

The battered moon on the slope
lay like a dune of sand;

and in the trap at my feet
the rabbit leapt and prayed
weeping blood, and crouched
when the light shone on the blade.

The sudden sun lit up
the webs from wire to wire;
the white webs, the white dew
blazed with a holy fire.

Flame of light in the dew,
flame of blood on the bush,
answered the whirling sun
and the voice of the early thrush.

I think of this for you.
I would not have you believe
the world is empty of truth,
or that men must grieve;

but hear the song of the martyrs
out of a bush of fire:
"All is consumed with love;
all is renewed with desire."

The Ancestors

That stream ran through the sunny grass so clear—
more polished than dew is, all one lilt of light.
We found our way up to the source, where stand
the fern-trees locked in endless age
under the smothering vine and the trees' night.

Their slow roots spread in mud and stone,
and in each notched trunk, shaggy as an ape,
crouches the ancestor, the dark bent foetus;
unopened eyes, face fixed in unexperienced sorrow,
and body contorted in the fern-tree's shape.

That sad, pre-history, unexpectant face—
I hear the answering sound of my blood, I know
these primitive fathers waiting for rebirth,
these children not yet born—the womb holds so
the moss-grown patience of the skull,
the old ape-knowledge of the embryo.

Their silent sleep is gathered round the spring
that feeds the living, thousand-lighted stream
up which we toiled into this timeless dream.

Two Songs for the World's End

I

Bombs ripen on the leafless tree
under which the children play,
and there my darling all alone
dances in the spying day.

I gave her nerves to feel her pain;
I put her mortal beauty on.
I taught her love, that hate might find
its black work the easier done.

I sent her out alone to play:
and I must watch, and I must hear,
how underneath the leafless tree
the children sing and dance with Fear.

II

Lighted by the rage of time
where the blind and dying weep,
in my shadow take your sleep;
though wakeful I.

Sleep unhearing while I pray—
Should the red tent of the sky
fall to fold your time away,
wake and weep before you die.

Die believing all is true
that love your maker said to you.
Still believe
that had you lived you would have found
love, world, sight, sound,
sorrow, beauty—all true.
Grieve for death your moment; grieve.

The world, the lover you must take,
is the murderer you will meet;
but if you die before you wake,
never think death sweet.

The Lost Man

To reach the pool you must go through the rain-forest—
through the bewildering midsummer of darkness
lit with ancient fern,
laced with poison and thorn.
You must go by the way he went—the way of the bleeding
hands and feet, the blood on the stones like flowers,
under the hooded flowers
that fall on the stones like blood.

To reach the pool you must go by the black valley,
among the crowding columns made of silence,
under the hanging clouds
of leaves and voiceless birds.
To go by the way he went to the voice of the water,
where the priest stinging-tree waits with his whips and
    fevers,
under the hooded flowers
that fall from the trees like blood,
you must forget the song of the gold bird dancing
over tossed light; you must remember nothing
except the drag of darkness
that draws your weakness under.
To go by the way he went, you must find beneath you
that last and faceless pool, and fall. And falling
find between breath and death
the sun by which you live.

The Traveller and the Angel

When I came to the strength of my youth
I set out on my journey;
and on the far side of the ford
the angel waited.

His voice—himself invisible—
rang through my carefree thought:
"I am the first of your tasks.
Learn now your own strength."

And his hand on my shoulder
was like an awakening—
the challenge of his touch lit up
delight on delight in me.

How long it was that we wrestled
I hardly know—time waited
while through defeat on defeat
I reached my triumph.

Full-tested, the pride of my youth,
strained to each farthest limit,
found its strength made greater,
its courage tried and proved;

and all that fight was joy.
Shall I ever know joy fiercer?—
feeling the subtle angel
shift from one trial to another.

Marvellously and matched like lovers,
we fought there by the ford;
till, every truth elicited,
I, unsurpassably weary,

felt with that weariness
darkness increase on my sight,
and felt the angel failing
in his glorious strength.

Altering, dissolving, vanishing,
he slipped through my fingers,
till when I groped for the death-blow,
I groped and could not find him.

But his voice on the air
pierced the depths of my heart.
"I was your strength; our battle
leaves you doubly strong.

"Now the way is open
and you must rise and find it—
the way to the next ford
where waits the second angel."

65

But weak with loss and fear
I lie still by the ford.
Now that the angel is gone,
I am a man, and weary.

Return, angel, return.
I fear the journey.

The Gateway

Through the gateway of the dead
(the traveller is speaking)
I kept my pride.
Stepping between those awful pillars
I knew that I myself
had imagined, acted,
and foreseen everything as it was here.

In the land of oblivion,
among black-mouthed ghosts,
I knew my Self
the sole reality.

But this was not permitted;
the way went farther.
Stepping down
by the shadows of the river,
even that river
(soundless, invisible)
vanished; and the path dissolved,
and I, upon it.

Self, my justification,
sole lover, sole companion,
slipped from my side.

To say that I recall that time,
that country,
would be a lie; time was not,
and I nowhere.
Yet two things remain—
one was the last surrender,
the other the last peace.
In the depths of nothing
I found my home.

All ended there,
yet all began.
All sank in dissolution
and rose renewed.

And the bright smoke
out of the pit of chaos
is the flowing and furious world.

And the mind's nightmare
is the world's sweet wellspring
(the traveller said).

FROM
THE TWO FIRES

The Two Fires

Among green shades and flowering ghosts, the
    remembrances of love,
inventions of the holy unwearying seed,
bright falling fountains made of time, that bore
through time the holy seed that knew no time—
I tell you, ghosts in the ghosts of summer days,
you are dead as though you never had been.
For time has caught on fire, and you too burn:
leaf, stem, branch, calyx and the bright corolla
are now the insubstantial wavering fire
in which love dies: the final pyre
of the beloved, the bridegroom and the bride.
These two we have denied.

In the beginning was the fire:
out of the death of fire, rock and the waters;
and out of water and rock, the single spark, the divine truth.
Far, far below, the millions of rock-years divide
to make a place for those who were born and died
to build the house that held the bridegroom and the bride.
Those two, who reigned in passion in the flower,
whom still the hollow seasons celebrate,
no ritual now can recreate.
Whirled separate in the man-created fire
their cycles end, with the cycle of the holy seed;
the cycle from the first to the last fire.
These too time can divide;
these too have died.

And walking here among the dying centuries—
the centuries of moss, of fern, of cycad,
of the towering tree—the centuries of the flower—
I pause where water falls from the face of the rock.
My father rock, do you forget the kingdom of the fire?
The aeons grind you into bread—
into the soil that feeds the living and transforms the dead;

and have we eaten in the heart of the yellow wheat
the sullen unforgetting seed of fire?

And now, set free by the climate of man's hate,
that seed sets time ablaze.
The leaves of fallen years, the forest of living days,
have caught like matchwood. Look, the whole world burns.
The ancient kingdom of the fire returns.
And the world, that flower that housed the bridegroom and
    the bride,
burns on the breast of night.
The world's denied.

The Precipice

At last it came into her mind, the answer.
She dressed the children, went out and hailed the driver.
There she sat holding them, looking through the window;
behaving like any woman; but she was no longer living.

To blame her would mean little; she had her logic,
the contained logic of a bomb, not even tragic,
to which each day had made its small addition
ending at last in this, which was completion.

There was no moon but she had brought her torch,
and the dark of the mountain forest opened like flesh
before her purpose; possessed and intent as any lover
she fled along the path, the children with her.

So reaching the edge at last and no less certain
she took the children in her arms because she loved them,
and jumped, parting the leaves and the night's curtain.

Now, and for years to come, that path is seared
by the blazing headlong torrent of their direction;

and we must hold our weathercock minds from turning
into its downward gale towards destruction.

Return

A far-off boat moves on the morning sea.
That broad and equal monotone of light
is drawn to focus; purpose enters in.
Its unity becomes duality,
and action scars perfection like a pin.

The mind in contemplation sought its peace—
that round and calm horizon's purity,
which, known one instant, must subsist always.
But life breaks in again, time does not cease;
that calm lies quiet under storms of days.

So moves in me time's purpose, evil and good.
Those silent tracts eternity may give,
but the lame shadow stumbles at my back,
still sick for love; the battle of flesh and blood
will hardly come to quiet while I live.

The Man Beneath the Tree

Nothing is so far as truth;
nothing is so plain to see.
Look where light has married earth
through the green leaves on the tree.

Nothing is so hard as love—
love for which the wisest weep;

yet the child who never looked
found it easily as his sleep.

Nothing is as strange as love—
love is like a foreign land.
Yet its natives find their way
natural as hand-in-hand.

Nothing is so bare as truth—
that lean geometry of thought;
but round its poles there congregate
all foliage, flowers and fruits of earth.

Oh, love and truth and I should meet,
sighed the man beneath the tree;
but where should our acquaintance be?
Between your hat and the soles of your feet,
sang the bird on top of the tree.

For Precision

Yet I go on from day to day, betraying
the core of light, the depth of darkness—
my speech inexact, the note not right,
never quite sure what I am saying—

on the periphery of truth. Uphold me now,
pure colours, blacks, whites, bells on the central tone,
middays, midnights. I wander among cross-lights.
Let me be sure and economical as the rayed
suns, stars, flowers, wheels; let me fall as a gull, a hawk,

through the confusions of foggy talk,
and pin with one irremediable stroke—
what?—the escaping wavering wandering light,
the blur, the brilliance; forming into one chord

what's separate and distracted; making the vague hard—
catching the wraith—speaking with a pure voice,
and that the gull's sole note like a steel nail
that driven through cloud, sky, and irrelevant seas,
joins all, gives all a meaning, makes all whole.

Nameless Flower

Three white petals float
above the green.
You cannot think they spring from it
till the fine stem's seen.

So separated each from each,
and each so pure,
yet at the centre here they touch
and form a flower.

Flakes that drop at the flight of a bird
and have no name,
I'll set a word upon a word
to be your home.

Up from the dark and jungle floor
you have looked long.
Now I come to lock you here
in a white song.

Word and word are chosen and met.
Flower, come in.
But before the trap is set,
the prey is gone.

The words are white as a stone is white
carved for a grave;
but the flower blooms in immortal light,
being now; being love.

Breath

I turned to the dark window;
outside were stars and frost.
My breath went out to the night,
shaped like a cloud or a mist.
Small and soulless ghost,
what was it my heart meant
that, watching the way you went,
it moved so under my breast?

Scribbly-gum

The cold spring falls from the stone.
I passed and heard
the mountain, palm and fern
spoken in one strange word.
The gum-tree stands by the spring.
I peeled its splitting bark
and found the written track
of a life I could not read.

Gum-trees Stripping

Say the need's born within the tree,
and waits a trigger set for light;
say sap is tidal like the sea
and rises with the solstice-heat—
but wisdom shells the words away
to watch this fountain slowed in air
where sun joins earth—to watch the place
at which these silent rituals are.

Words are not meanings for a tree.
So it is truer not to say
"These rags look like humility,
or this year's wreck of last year's love,
or wounds ripped by the summer's claw."
If it is possible to be wise
here, wisdom lies outside the word
in the earlier answer of the eyes.

Wisdom can see the red, the rose,
the stained and sculptured curve of grey,
the charcoal scars of fire, and see
around that living tower of tree
the hermit tatters of old bark
split down and strip to end the season;
and can be quiet and not look
for reasons past the edge of reason.

Seven Songs for a Journey

I *Carnarvon Range*

Carnarvon Creek
and cliffs of Carnarvon,
your tribes are silent;
I will sing for you—
each phrase
the size of a stone—
a red stone,
a white stone,
a grey,
and a purple;
a parrot's cry
from a blossoming tree,
a scale of water
and wavering light—

each word a sign
to set on your cliffs,
each phrase a stone
to lie in your waters.

A white orchid
from the cave's shade,
a fish from your waters
clearer than green—
I shall take these two
in exchange for a song,
Carnarvon Creek
and cliffs of Carnarvon.

II *Brigalow Country*

When the metal-blue moon
plays tunes on the hut roof,
and the long slope darkens
with its brigalow tribe,
then Margery dances,
awkward as an emu—
dances for the useless
coin of the moon.

Haunted and alone
with the tribe of the brigalows,
their steel-coloured leaves
as curved as a skinning-knife,
her sidelong eye
as queer as the moonlight,
Margery dances
to the singing of the dingoes.

Living lost and lonely
with the tribe of the brigalows,
don't want to stay
but never can go.
Never get no money

for when I go hungry,
never get no kisses
for when I feel sad—
rooted like the brigalows
until I'm dead.

When the bright tin moon
plays tunes on the hut-roof,
Margery dances
in her long pale hair.
And the tribe of the brigalows
drop their shadows
like still black water,
and watch her there.

III *Night*

The contours of night are like
the contours of this rock,
and worn by light as by water.

The pin-sharp stars drag
their thin bright trails across it.
The moon's pale creek and the floods
of the sunlight erode it;
and round its secret flanks
the currents of the living—
plant, beast, man and god—
swirl their phosphorescence.

Night is what remains
when the equation is finished.
Night is the earth's dream
that the sun is dead.
Night is man's dream
that he has invented God—
the dream of before-creation;
the dream of falling.

Night blocks our way, saying,
I at least am real.

The contours of night are like
the contours of this rock.

IV *The Prospector*

Full moon's too bright for sleeping;
I'll watch her rise
on the range where no bird's speaking
except in the crow's voice—
on the land to be won by love only;
and here there's none
but the fire's black kiss, and the lonely
print of skull and bone.

Rise up and walk, old skeleton.
But no; lie still.
Let no phase of the moon disturb you,
no heats recall.
Let the bones dream on, the kind dream
that was their last—
dream the mirage's river
has quenched the world's thirst.

Full moon's too bright for sleeping—
too white the sky.
And foreign to this country
restless I lie.
But you, moon, you're no stranger:
you're known here, moon,
drawing your mad hands over
rock, dust and bone.

V *Canefields Country*

The coloured girl leans on the bridge,
folding her sorrow into her breast.

Her face is a dark and downward mirror
where her eyes look, and are lost.

The old land is marshalled under
the heavy regiment of green cane;
but by the lagoon the paperbarks
unroll their blank and tattered parchment,
waiting for some unknown inscription
which love might make in ink-dark water.

And in that water the great lily
sets her perfect dusk-blue petals
in their inherited order of prayer
around that blazing throne, her centre.
There time shall meet eternity
and their worship find its answer.

VI *Sea-beach*

Mountain, wall and tree
bear witness against our lives,
being scrawled with obsolete slogans
initialled by clumsy knives—
no one has marked the sea.

Below high tide you can stand
as though you stood in the sky.
No sign on the clean sand
will stay to remember you by.

Sea, anonymous pilgrim
made free of time and place,
from the unhistoried poles
and the shores of Asia and Greece

you carry no memory,
you bear nò symbol or gift,
except the unshaped bone,
the silver splinter of raft.

And though you beckon and play
we will not stay here long.
We will snatch back the child
who trusts too far to your song.

The sea cleans everything,
a sailor said to me:
and these white empty shells
come out of the scour of the sea.

VII *Mount Mary*

The solitary mountain is as tall as grief—
a figure in an estranged landscape, drawing
her biblical blue cloak across her shoulders.
Age and the sun have worn her barren;
even the one small creek of her tears is drying;
and the crows haunt her, crying her name,
like birds blackened by hell-fire, crying and flying.

The mountain sits among rocks, and over her head
noonday's white skull-moon hangs dead.
Nothing is left for her to dream on, virgin
and widow, except the few small pools of her tears,
rock-bound and sunk, that will not reach the sea.

But by those pools I found two trees in flower
One wept long branches full of withering stars,
and one, naked of leaves, held up a crown:
a great fierce blossom yellow as the sun
taken out of the sky at his heat's thirsty noon.

81

Sanctuary

The road beneath the giant original trees
sweeps on and cannot wait. Varnished by dew,
its darkness mimics mirrors and is bright
behind the panic eyes the driver sees
caught in headlights. Behind his wheels the night
takes over: only the road ahead is true.
It knows where it is going; we go too.

Sanctuary, the sign said. Sanctuary—
trees, not houses; flat skins pinned to the road
of possum and native-cat; and here the old tree stood
for how many thousand years? that old gnome-tree
some axe-new boy cut down. Sanctuary, it said:
but only the road has meaning here. It leads
into the world's cities like a long fuse laid.

Fuse, nerve, strand of a net, tense
bearer of messages, snap-tight violin-string,
dangerous knife-edge laid across the dark,
what has that sign to do with you? The immense
tower of antique forest and cliff, the rock
where years accumulate like leaves, the tree
where transient bird and mindless insect sing?
The word the board holds up is Sanctuary,
and the road knows that notice-boards make sense,

but has no time to pray. Only, up there,
morning sets doves upon the power-line.
Swung on that fatal voltage like a sign
and meaning love, perhaps they are a prayer.

At Cooloolah

The blue crane fishing in Cooloolah's twilight
has fished there longer than our centuries.
He is the certain heir of lake and evening,
and he will wear their colour till he dies;

but I'm a stranger, come of a conquering people.
I cannot share his calm, who watch his lake,
being unloved by all my eyes delight in
and made uneasy, for an old murder's sake.

Those dark-skinned people who once named Cooloolah
knew that no land is lost or won by wars,
for earth is spirit; the invader's feet will tangle
in nets there and his blood be thinned by fears.

Riding at noon and ninety years ago,
my grandfather was beckoned by a ghost—
a black accoutred warrior armed for fighting,
who sank into bare plain, as now into time past.

White shores of sand, plumed reed and paperbark,
clear heavenly levels frequented by crane and swan—
I know that we are justified only by love,
but oppressed by arrogant guilt, have room for none.

And walking on clean sand among the prints
of bird and animal, I am challenged by a driftwood spear
thrust from the water; and, like my grandfather,
must quiet a heart accused by its own fear.

Landscapes

To look at landscapes loved by the newly dead
is to move into the dark and out again.
Every brilliant leaf that lives by light
dies from its hold at last and desires earth's bed:
men and trees and grasses daily falling
make that veil of beauty for her. Slight
aeons of soil on rock, of grass on soil, of men
standing on grass, can't hide her outcrops. Stone—
stone our mother locks in, tongueless, without feeling,
our far blind brothers, future, and past who had no luck
and never was born. And now the newly dead
is lowered there. Now we weep for eyes whose look
is closed on landscapes loved, and at last known.

. . . and Mr Ferritt

But now Mr Ferritt
with his troublesome nose,
with his shaven chin
and his voice like a grief
that grates in dark corners,
moves in his house
and scrapes his dry skin
and sees it is morning.

O day, you sly thief,
now what have you taken
of all the small things
I tie on my life?
The radio serial
whines in the kitchen,
caught in a box,
and cannot get out.

The finch in his cage,
the border of phlox
as straight as a string
drawn up in my garden,
the potted geranium,
all are there.
But day from his cranium
twitches one hair;
and never again
will a hair grow there.
—O day, you sly thief,
how you pluck at my life,
frets Mr Ferritt;
but there, he must bear it.

Outside the fence
the wattle-tree grows.
It tosses, it shines,
it speaks its one word.
Beware, beware!
Mr Ferritt has heard.
—What are axes for?
What are fences for?
Who planted that wattle-tree
right at my door?
God only knows.
All over the garden
its dust is shaken.
No wonder I sneeze
as soon as I waken.

O world, you sly thief,
my youth you have taken,
and what have you given
who promised me heaven,
but a nagging wife
and a chronic catarrh,
and a blonde on the pictures
as far as a star?

And wild and gold
as a film-star's hair
that tree stands there,
blocking the view
from my twenty-perch block.
What are axes for?
What are fences for,
but to keep this tree
away from my door?

And down came the tree.
But poor Mr Ferritt
still has hay-fever.
Nothing will cure it.

Flesh

I *The Hand*

Put your hand out, and hold it still, and look.
Like something wild picked up and held too long,
it loses truth: light fades on the stopped wing.
Infinite cleverness pivoted on a clever stalk,
it lives in time and space, and there is strong;
but draw it outside doing into being,
it pales and withers like a sea-star dying.

The hand is drawn from the flesh by its own uses.
Powers unchannelled, shapes unshaped await it,
and what has long since happened and been completed
lies in it and directs its bone and chooses
stress and muscle. Textures thrust to meet it,
for it is their answer; stuff that cannot move
moves under the hand that is all it knows of love.

Do not look at me, the hand says. I am not true
except as means. I am the road, the bridge,
not starting-point nor goal nor traveller.
I am not you, the doer, nor what you do.
I am extension: I am your farthest edge.
I am that which strokes the child's hair tenderly—tenderly—
and drives the nail into the hand stretched on the tree.
My shape is action. Look away. Do not look at me.

II *The Body*

I am the depth below. You would do well
to look down, sometimes. I can be your tree,
solid in the gale—if you consent to be flower,
seed, and fruit. But you don't believe in me
except as crass and suffering and to be suffered,
or instrument of your uncertain love.

I am your notion of hell
and your tool for discovering heaven. But perched on me
you lean out with your arrogant polished eye—
trying to be God. Look down; remember where you are.
I am the strata that reach from earth to star
and the great cliff down which your father Adam fell.

You would do well to look down.
More was built into me than quickset night.
God walked through all my ages. He set in me
the key that fits the keyhole; use it right
and eternity's lightning splits the rock of time.
And there I was begun and so begotten
in that unspeakable heart of flame.
From that light where flesh on flesh was welded
the world itself unfolded.
Look down through me on the light you have forgotten.

I am your blundering kind companion.
I am your home that keeps out bitter weather.
I am the perilous slow deposit of time's wisdom.

87

You are my threat, my murder. And yet remember,
I am yourself. Come, let us live together.

III *The Face*

The face turns inward and down
on the head's bud;
curves to its inner world
of shaping flesh and blood:
is closed like an eyelid; blind;
is made before its mind.

Birth draws the stalk out straight
and the face wakes.
Naked in a passion of light
its long composure breaks.
It writhes to regain sleep;
but life has stung too deep,

and flesh has now become
time's instrument
for the first task that is set
and the easiest learnt.
Two shapes obsess it: need,
and the need satisfied.

The mirror answers the face:
an animal in a cave
that lusts and tastes and sings.
A hill that breathes the air;
a glance that looks for love;
two crystals where all things
leech at the panes and stare.

What shall the face pursue
that drinks of time and event
and changes as it drinks?
What was it the flesh meant
foreshadowing in the womb
the person not yet come?

The face that turns to the world
opens itself to ask.
Look at it now, before
it learns it is a mask:
for eyes take light like dew
while their glance is new.

It takes out of the air
all it can know.
Whatever look turns on it,
that look it will grow.
So some learn love, and some
can never find a home.

The face becomes its world.
It is the moving field
printed by days grown common
and the unmastered night—
by unacknowledged need,
and fear of its own deed;

yet knows that there have been,
flowering the world's dull years,
faces more true than stars
and made of purer light;
and they may happen again.
O may they happen again.

The Cup

Silence is harder, Una said.
If I could be quiet I might come true
like the blue cup hung over the sink,
which is not dead,
but waiting for someone to fill it and drink.

Una said, Silence can reach my mouth;
but a long way in my trouble lies.
The look in my eyes, the sound of my words,
all tell the truth:
they spring from my trouble like a flight of birds.

Let silence travel, Una said,
by every track of nerve and vein
to heart and brain, where the troubles begin.
Then I shan't be dead,
but waiting for something to come in.

An Old Man

Old Gustav sings on Endless Creek,
"The spotted-gums are stripping down,
the yellow box in flower again;
all as it was in the old joy
that time first made when time was long
and I a boy—and I a boy.

"Love is various as the sea,
and many shapes can death put on.
May not the white-ant love the tree?
and the strangler-fig has a woman's arms.
Whatever made the world, it seems,
will not change till time is done.

"As innocent as the yellow-box flower,
as deadly as the brown snake's fang,
it has the thunder's word to speak
and the weebill's tiny song.
It grows in me with sorrow and joy.
It sets the cancer in my side.
And it will bring, when I have died,

the box to flower on Endless Creek
as once it flowered, and I a boy."

In Praise of Marriages

Not till life halved, and parted
one from the other,
did time begin, and knowledge;
sorrow, delight.
Terror of being apart, being lost,
made real the night.
Seeking and finding made
yesterday, now and tomorrow;
and love was realized first
when those two came together.

So, perilously joined,
lighted in one small room,
we have made all things true.
Out of the I and the you
spreads this field of power,
that all that waits may come,
all possibles be known—
all futures step from their stone
and pasts come into flower.

Request to a Year

If the year is meditating a suitable gift,
I should like it to be the attitude
of my great-great-grandmother,
legendary devotee of the arts,

who, having had eight children
and little opportunity for painting pictures,
sat one day on a high rock
beside a river in Switzerland,

and from a difficult distance viewed
her second son, balanced on a small ice-floe,
drift down the current towards a waterfall
that struck rock-bottom eighty feet below,

while her second daughter, impeded,
no doubt, by the petticoats of the day,
stretched out a last-hope alpenstock
(which luckily later caught him on his way).

Nothing, it was evident, could be done;
and with the artist's isolating eye
my great-great-grandmother hastily sketched the scene.
The sketch survives to prove the story by.

Year, if you have no Mother's Day present planned,
reach back and bring me the firmness of her hand.

Storm

On the headland's grassed and sheltered side,
out of the wind I crouch and watch
while driven by the seaward ship-destroying storm
races of insane processional breakers come.
A long-dead divine authority reflows the tide
at evening, and already the gnawed hill of beach
alters and shrinks. The waves cry out: Let us be done.

Let us be done with the long submission, the whips
that hurl us for ever on time's frigid stone
mouthing our ever-repeated plea for an answer and getting
    none.

Let us break free, smash down the land's gate
and drown all questions under a black flood.
Hate, then, the waves cry; hate.

And round each headland of the world, each drenching
    rock,
crowding each wild spray-drop, as in the womb's calm lying,
they beat and whirl on the waves, the invisible legion
of momentary crystals, less-than-a-second's-tick
lives, love's first and everywhere creation;
so small, so strong, that nothing of this mad rock-torn
surge and violence, not the storm's final desperation
touches them,
busy in the unhurt stillness, breeding and dying.

Song

O where does the dancer dance—
the invisible centre spin—
whose bright periphery holds
the world we wander in?

For it is he we seek—
the source and death of desire;
we blind as blundering moths
around that core of fire.

Caught between birth and death
we stand alone in the dark,
to watch the blazing wheel
on which the earth is a spark,

crying, Where does the dancer dance—
the terrible centre spin,
whose flower will open at last
to let the wanderer in?

Wildflower Plain

The angry granite,
the hungry range,
must crumble away,
must melt and change;
forget the single
iron word
that no voice spoke
when no ear heard,
and learn this thorny,
delicate, tender
speech of the flower
as last surrender:
this various speech
that covers over
the gravel plain
like the words of a lover.

Blue orchid gentle
as skies seen early;
blown purple iris
so quick to wither;
tea-tree falling
on water-lily;
heath, boronia,
many another,
can but spring
where rock makes way.
Let rock be humble.
Let it decay.
Let time's old anger
become new earth,
to sign to the heart
the truth of death.

The Harp and the King

Old king without a throne,
the hollow of despair
behind his obstinate unyielding stare,
knows only, God is gone;
and, fingers clenching on his chair,
feels night and the soul's terror coming on.

Bring me that harp, that singer. Let him sing.
Let something fill the space inside the mind,
that's a dry stream-bed for the flood of fear.
Song's only sound; but it's a lovely sound,
a fountain through the drought. Bring David here,
said the old frightened king.

Sing something. Comfort me.
Make me believe the meaning in the rhyme.
The world's a traitor to the self-betrayed;
but once I thought there was a truth in time,
while now my terror is eternity.
So do not take me outside time.
Make me believe in my mortality,
since that is all I have, the old king said.

I sing the praise of time, the harp replied:
the time of aching drought when the black plain
cannot believe in roots or leaves or rain.
Then lips crack open in the stone-hard peaks,
and rock begins to suffer and to pray,
when all that lives has died
and withered in the wind and blown away,
and earth has no more strength to bleed.

I sing the praise of time and of the rain—
the word creation speaks.
Four elements are locked in time;
the sign that makes them fertile is the seed,

and this outlasts all death and springs again,
the running water of the harp-notes cried.

But the old king sighed obstinately,
How can that comfort me?
Night and the terror of the soul come on,
and out of me both water and seed have gone.
What other generations shall I see?
But make me trust my failure and my fall,
said the sad king, since these are now my all.

I sing the praise of time, the harp replied.
In time we fail, alone with hours and tears,
ruin our followers and traduce our cause,
and give our love its last and fatal hurt.
In time we fail and fall.
In time the company even of God withdraws,
and we are left with our own murderous heart.

Yet it is time that holds,
somewhere although not now,
the peal of trumpets for us; time that bears,
made fertile even by these tears,
even by this darkness, even by this loss,
incredible redemptions—hours that grow,
as trees grow fruit, in a blind holiness,
the truths unknown, the loves unloved by us.

But the old king turned his head sullenly.
How can that comfort me
who see into the heart as deep as God can see?
Love's sown in us; perhaps it flowers; it dies.
I failed my God and I betrayed my love.
Make me believe in treason; that is all I have.

This is the praise of time, the harp cried out—
that we betray all truths that we possess.
Time strips the soul and leaves it comfortless
and sends it thirsty through a bone-white drought.

Time's subtler treacheries teach us to betray.
What else could drive us on our way?
Wounded we cross the desert's emptiness
and must be false to what would make us whole.
For only change and distance shape for us
some new tremendous symbol for the soul.

FROM
BIRDS

The Peacock

Shame on the aldermen who locked
the Peacock in a dirty cage!
His blue and copper sheens are mocked
by habit, hopelessness and age.

The weary Sunday families
along their gravelled paths repeat
the pattern of monotonies
that he treads out with restless feet.

And yet the Peacock shines alone;
and if one metal feather fall
another grows where that was grown.
Love clothes him still, in spite of all.
How pure the hidden spring must rise
that time and custom cannot stain!
It speaks its joy again—again.
Perhaps the aldermen are wise.

Extinct Birds

Charles Harpur in his journals long ago
(written in hope and love, and never printed)
recorded the birds of his time's forest—
birds long vanished with the fallen forest—
described in copperplate on unread pages.

The scarlet satin-bird, swung like a lamp in berries,
he watched in love, and then in hope described it.
There was a bird, blue, small, spangled like dew.
All now are vanished with the fallen forest.
And he, unloved, past hope, was buried,

who helped with proud stained hands to fell the forest,
and set those birds in love on unread pages;
yet thought himself immortal, being a poet.
And is he not immortal, where I found him,
in love and hope along his careful pages?—
the poet vanished, in the vanished forest,
among his brightly tinted extinct birds?

Brush Turkey

Right to the edge of his forest
the tourists come.
He learns the scavenger's habits
with scrap and crumb—
his forests shrunk, he lives
on what the moment gives:
pretends, in mockery,
to beg our charity.

Cunning and shy one must be
to snatch one's bread
from oafs whose hands are quicker
with stones instead.
He apes the backyard bird;
half-proud and half-absurd,
sheltered by his quick wit,
he sees and takes his bit.

Ash-black, wattles of scarlet
and careful eye,
he hoaxes the ape, the ogre,
with mimicry.
Scornfully, he will eat
thrown crust and broken meat
till suddenly—"See, oh see!
The turkey's in the tree."

The backyard bird is stupid;
he trusts and takes.
But this one's wiles are wary
to guard against the axe:
escaping, neat and pat,
into his habitat.
Charred log and shade and stone
accept him. He is gone.

And here's a bird the poet
may ponder over,
whose ancient forest-meanings
no longer grant him cover;
who, circumspect yet proud,
like yet unlike the crowd,
must cheat its chucklehead
to throw, not stones, but bread.

FROM
THE FOREST

The Forest

When first I knew this forest
its flowers were strange.
Their different forms and faces
changed with the seasons' change—

white violets smudged with purple,
the wild-ginger spray,
ground-orchids small and single
haunted my day;

the thick-fleshed Murray-lily,
flame-tree's bright blood,
and where the creek runs shallow,
the cunjevoi's green hood.

When first I knew this forest,
time was to spend,
and time's renewing harvest
could never reach an end.

Now that its vines and flowers
are named and known,
like long-fulfilled desires
those first strange joys are gone.

My search is further.
There's still to name and know
beyond the flowers I gather
that one that does not wither—
the truth from which they grow.

Five Senses

Now my five senses
gather into a meaning
all acts, all presences;
and as a lily gathers
the elements together,
in me this dark and shining,
that stillness and that moving,
these shapes that spring from nothing,
become a rhythm that dances,
a pure design.

While I'm in my five senses
they send me spinning
all sounds and silences,
all shape and colour
as thread for that weaver,
whose web within me growing
follows beyond my knowing
some pattern sprung from nothing—
a rhythm that dances
and is not mine.

The Nautilus

Some queer unshaped uncoloured animal,
much like a moment's pause of smoke or mist,
was yet so made that nothing less
than this hard perfect shape involving it
would do to speak its meaning in the world.

Out of its birth it came with this.
The smallest spiral holds the history
of something tiny in the battering sea,

that carried on its obstinate gathering,
till the years swelled in it to one last perfect
ballooning curve of colour laid by colour.
All was implicit in its hold on time.

Say that the thing was slave to its own meaning
and the unconscious labour of its body.
The terms were these, that it could never guess
how it conspired with time to shroud itself—
a splendid action common to its kind
but never known in doing.

Not even the end of making gave the meaning.
The thing it made was its own self, enclosed it,
and was the prison that prevented sight.
Yet though death strands its emptied spiral,
this sweet completion puts a term to time;
and that, I take it, was the bargain.

Praise for the Earth

The writer in the lighted room
is not single nor alone:
but let him drop his pen and turn
and see the towering universe
wheel its faint lights in the far gloom,
then all the work that time has done
still leaves the heart companionless.

So gather in the golden dead
till all we own is harvested.
While world's our own and our heart's food,
no need to fear eternity.
Little the time that's left for love
between the poised and the broken wave;
let us, who hang like a wave on the sea,
praise all the dead and all who live.

Q to A

Oh why so fill me
with such delight and terror,
only to leave me
empty of all but sorrow?
       It was my pleasure.

Once you replied
most clear and ever truthful,
who now are silent.
Must I alone be faithful?
       Your question is your answer.

Was I deceived then,
and was it my own echo
I heard and loved then?
My heart is woe to fear so.
       Where found you then your treasure?

In love, it was in love
I found my rest,
And that my own heart gave.
       Put there your trust.

The Lake

All day the candid staring of the lake
holds what's passing and forgets the past.
Faithful to cloud and leaf, not knowing leaf nor cloud,
it spreads its smooth eye wide for something's sake.
All daylight's there; and all the night at last
drops threads of light from star to under-star.

Eye of the earth, my meaning's what you are.
You see no tree nor cloud. That's what I take

out of your waters in this net I cast—
the net where time is knotted by the word,
that flying needle. Lakes and eyes at last
drain dry, but the net-maker still must make.

What lover's shuttle flew when all began?
Who chose the images this net can draw?—
sun, moon and cloud, the hanging leaves and trees,
and leaning through, the terrible face of man:
my face. I looked, and there my eyes met eyes,
lover to lover. Deep I looked, and saw.

Interplay

What is within becomes what is around.
This angel morning on the world-wild sea
is seared with light that's mine and comes from me,
and I am mirror to its blaze and sound,
as lovers double in their interchange.

Yet I am not the seer, nor world the sight;
I am transcended by a single word—
Let there be light—and all creation stirred.
I am that cry alone, that visioned light,
its voice and focus. It's the word that's strange.

Look how the stars' bright chaos eddies in
to form our constellations. Flame by flame
answers the ordering image in the name.
World's signed with words; there light—there love begin.

Dry Storm

The uninhabited mountains stand up green,
naked with rock or clothed with an old forest
where vines and thorns tangle in damp and dark
among the trunks and boulders. Curls of fern
and coils of water over leaves and rock
pattern the snake's long body, hide from harm
moth, bird and lizard. From those ancient turrets
tonight thrusts up the cloud of this dry storm.

Spring's months are thirsty. The valley's crops are sown
and the seed waits. But nothing comes tonight
except the thrust of lightning. There is sound;
but it is thunder circling, here and gone,
and not the increasing rain. Long since it rained,
and now the grass is dry, ready to burn,
and farmers fear the lightning. The cloud's heart
is torn wide open, but it means no rain.

O ease our restlessness. Wild wandering dark,
vague hurrying depths of storm, pause and be full,
and thrust your fullness into our desire
till time release us, till we sleep. And wake
to a cool sky and a soaked earth left bare
to drink its light in peace.
                            But this storm's dry,
and dries us with its passion; and means ill,
reared from dark forests to a darker sky.

A Child's Nightmare

The holy image dwells within,
bequeathed by time from man to man.
It rages in us while we can

109

support its fires and yet not burn.
And children learn, as the years pass,
the char of that insatiate flame
that melts the towering universe
into a symbol and a name.

Earth is a sad yet glittering star.
Bodied in beast and man and bird,
she seeks her vision and her fear,
old Chaos and the shaping Word;
and we who travel on her path
hold ecstasy and nightmare both.

So you come running from your dreams
where flame and shadow one by one
reveal and darken all that's known,
to sob and tremble in my arms.

Bachelor Uncle

When you came visiting
the house was sour and strange.
Time past was all betrayed
by unknown youth and change.
And in the children's glance
that turned from you and ran,
you saw instead of yourself
an empty cross old man,
alien, denied by all
but the old clocks on the wall.
Ticking as brittle and dry
as an ageing artery
they spoke time's cruelty.

So you took down each clock,
undid its insect-shell,

till spring and coil and wheel
littered your room's cold cell;
and, disarticulate,
old time your enemy
ran mad with chime and bell
of sick machinery.
And day by day you sat
intent and desolate,
with sharpened lip and eye—
an old clock gone awry.

Then it was time to pack—
time to be gone again.
You put the wheels together,
oiled them all with a feather,
and set and took them back.
Time's true and must be told
to the meticulous second;
and your week's work was reckoned
a service due to pride,
neat-handed though grown old.

The Graves at Mill Point

Alf Watt is in his grave
These eighty years.
From his bones a bloodwood grows
With long leaves like tears.

His girl grew weary long ago;
She's long lost the pain
Of crying to the empty air
To hold her boy again.

When he died the town died.
Nothing's left now

But the wind in the bloodwoods:
"Where did they go?

"In the rain beside the graves
I heard their tears say
—This is where the world ends;
The world ends today.

"Six men, seven men
Lie in one furrow.
The peaty earth goes over them,
But cannot blind our sorrow—"

"Where have they gone to?
I can't hear or see.
Tell me of the world's end,
You heavy bloodwood tree."

"There's nothing but a butcher-bird
Singing on my wrist,
And the long wave that rides the lake
With rain upon its crest.

"There's nothing but a wandering child
Who stoops to your stone;
But time has washed the words away,
So your story's done."

Six men, seven men
Are left beside the lake,
And over them the bloodwood tree
Flowers for their sake.

Old Woman's Song

The moon drained white by day
lifts from the hill

where the old pear-tree, fallen in storm,
puts out some blossom still.

Women believe in the moon.
This branch I hold
is not more white and still than she
whose flower is ages old;

and so I carry home
this branch of pear
that makes such obstinate tokens still
of fruit it cannot bear.

Age to Youth

The sooty bush in the park
is green as any forest
for the boy to lie beneath,
with his arms around his dearest;

the black of the back street
is washed as any cloud
when the girl and the boy
touch hands among the crowd.

No, nothing's better than love,
than to want and to hold:
it is wise in the young
to forget the common world:

to be lost in the flesh
and the light shining there:
not to listen to the old
whose tune is fear and care—

who tell them love's a drink
poisoned with sorrow,

the flesh a flower today
and withered by tomorrow.

It is wise in the young
to let heart go racing heart,
to believe that the earth
is young and safe and sweet;

and the message we should send
from age back to youth
is that every kiss and glance
is truer than the truth;

that whatever we repent
of the time that we live,
it is never what we give—
it is never that we love.

Double Image

The long-dead living forest rose
as white as bone, as dark as hair.
In rage the old protagonists
fought for my life; and I was there.

My kinsman's flesh, my kinsman's skull
enclosed me, and our wounds were one.
The long-dead forest reeled and sank
before that bitter night was done—

before we struck and tore again
the jumping flesh from out his hide,
and drank the blood that ran and slowed
to show the moment when he died.

O curve of horror in the claw,
and speech within the speechless eye—
when one must die, not knowing death,
and one knows death who cannot die.

They run from me, my child, my love,
when in those long-dead forests caught
I pace. My tears behind his eyes,
my kinsman dreams of what is not—

dreaming of knowledge and of love
in agony he treads his path.
I bud in him, a thorn, a pain,
and yet my nightmare holds us both.

I drink his murder's choking blood,
and he in ignorance sheds my tears.
The centuries bind us each in each—
the tongueless word, the ignorant ears.

Till from those centuries I wake,
naked and howling, still unmade,
within the forests of my heart
my dangerous kinsman runs afraid.

Judas in Modern Dress

Not like those men they tell of, who just as suddenly
walk out of life, from wife and fire and cooking-pot
and the whole confusion, to sit alone and naked
and move past motion; gaze through dark and day
with eyes that answer neither. Having completed their
    journey
they are free to travel past the end of journeys.
But I stepped out alone.
"I reject the journey; it was not I who chose it.

115

I worked for one end only,
to find the key that lets me through the door
marked Exit. I have found it and I use it."

There is a tale I heard a wise man tell,
how, tattered with age, beneath a fruiting tree
a seeker sat, and heard in God's great silence
another traveller, caught in the nets of self,
weeping between anguish and ecstasy,
and over a thousand miles stretched out one hand
to pluck him back again into the Way.

But I was one the saints knew not at all.
A mocking man, a sad man-animal
rejecting world and sense
not for God's love, but man's intelligence;
as though a hog looked through a human eye
and saw the human world as dunged as its own sty,
foul ante-room to death. Like that I saw
the abattoir ahead, and smelt the soil
soaked under me with blood. No place for me.

And wise in my own way I worked to find
the weak place in the palings of the Real—
the gap between the Word
and its Creation, the act and the conception—
and forced my way between those married two,
set time against eternity, struggled through,
slipped through annihilation, still being I.

What violence those great powers did to me
as I escaped between, I have forgotten.
But swinging clear I saw the world spin by
and leave me, empty as an insect-shell,
beyond the chance of death, and outside time.

I had the choice. Once I had infinite choices—
all the variety of light and shadow
that sprang to being when Choice first was made.

Now I have knowledge only. Knowledge, and eyes
to watch the worlds cross their eternities.

Times after times the saving word is spoken.
Times after times I feel it wither me.
The fools of time live on and never hear,
and I who hear have chosen not to answer.
It beats against me till my ears are broken.
Times after times I see my death go by
and cannot reach it even with a prayer.
Indeed, since I am neither Here nor There
I cannot live, and therefore cannot die.

Times after times my lips begin to form
the word that I renounced, and close again.
The worlds pass jostling, and their makers dream
immortal life betrayed to daily pain—
the pain that I denied.

I still deny it.

O sweet, sweet, sweet the love in human eyes—
the tree of blossom dressed to meet the bee,
all white, all radiant, golden at the heart.
Halt there, at your Creation! And it dies,
dies into rotting fruit, and tyrannous seed.
If it spring up again, so much the worse.
That was the curse on Eden, Adam's curse.
The curse by which my heart will not abide.

If I am Judas, still my cause is good.
I will not move my lips to answer God.

Vision

He who once saw that world beyond the world,
so that each tree and building, stone and face
cracked open like a mask before a flame
and showed the tree, the stone, the face behind it—
walked forever with that beatification.
Waking at night, against the blank of darkness,
knew he contained it; touched hand upon brow
and in his gladness cried "I, even I!"
—knowing the human ends in the divine.

Pride, greed, and ignorance—that world's three veils—
through them he walked and saw what lay beyond;
saw what the human eye was meant to see:
and watched the greedy and the stupid fumble
in a blind fear with intellect and pride—
those blades that cut the ignorant hands that hold them.
So he was sad for victim and oppressor,
for crying child and brute with the slack mouth,
for schemer, clod and safe respectable man
and all who had not seen what he had seen.

And yet these, too, moved in that second world
and stood up real behind the masks of hatred.
The very wound and weapon bled and glittered
as though both steel and flesh were made of light
and men the instruments in some high battle
where God incomprehensibly warred on God.

Wherefore he closed his eyes and hands, and prayed
vision and action know their proper limits,
and knowledge teach him more humility.

Moth

The great moth winged with many eyes
frets from his breast its silver dust.
Caught in the net my lamp has cast
he beats and circles till he dies.

His life was set on some true path
until his kind inhabited night
betrayed him to a craze of light,
light meaningless and cold like death—

or so I said, who watched him parch
upon his sterile radiant heaven—
a love unjoined, a gift ungiven—
strange failure in the eternal search:

and so turned back my pen to prayer
that might be language for a moth:
"O overcome me, Power and Truth;
transmute my ignorance, burn it bare;
so that against your flame, not I
but all that is not You, may die."

Reason and Unreason

When I began to test my heart,
its laws and fantasies, against the world,
the pain of impact made me sad.
Where heart was curved the world ran straight,
where it lay warm the world came cold.
It seemed my heart, or else the world, was mad.

Could I reject arithmetics,
their plain unanswerable arguings,

or find a cranny outside categories,
where two and two made soldiers, love or six?
My heart observed the silence round its songs,
the indifference that met its stories;

believed itself a changeling crazed,
and bowed its head to every claim of reason;
but then stood up and realized
when work is over love begins its season;
each day is contraried by night
and Caesar's coin is paid for Venus' rite;

and knew its fantasies, since time began,
outdone by earth's wild dreams, Plant, Beast and Man.

For My Daughter

The days begin to set
your difference in your face.
The world has caught you up
to go at the world's pace.
Time, that is not denied,
as once from my heart it drew
the blood that nourished you,
now draws you from my side.

My body gave you then
what was ordained to give,
and did not need my will.
But now we learn to live
apart, what must I do?
Out of my poverty
what new gift can there be
that I can find for you?

Love was our first exchange—
the kindness of the blood.
Animals know as much,
and know that it is good.
But when the child is grown
and the mouth leaves the breast,
such simple good is past
and leaves us more alone.

So we grow separate
and separate spend our days.
You must become your world
and follow in its ways;
but out of my own need,
not knowing where nor how,
I too must journey now
upon a different road.

While love is innocent
the lion walks beside.
But when the spell's undone
and where the paths divide,
he must be tamed, or slain,
or else the heart's undone.
The path I walk upon
leads to his den again.

When I shall meet with him
I pray to wrestle well;
I pray to learn the way
to tame him, not to kill.
Then he may be my friend,
as Una's once, in love,
and I shall understand
what gifts are mine to give.

Naming the Stars

Now all the garden's overcome with dark,
its flowers transplanted, low to high,
become night's far-off suns, and map in hand
we find where Sirius and Canopus stand
and trace our birth-stars on the zodiac.
Is it not strange that you and I
should write those names like jewels on the sky?

My Twins shine in the north, your red-eyed Bull
runs at Orion, each horn ablaze;
but who are we to claim them? Far and far
they fly, and no star sees his brother star;
not Castor knows his twin among them all,
and Taurus with his Pleiades
is the old figure of a dead man's gaze.

Yet they, like us, are caught in time and cause
and eddied on their single stream.
Earth watches through our eyes, and as we stare
she greets, by us, her far compatriots there,
the wildhaired Suns and the calm Wanderers.
Her ancient thought is marked in every name;
hero and creature mingle in her dream.

On her dark breast we spring like points of light
and set her language on the map of night.

Sports Field

Naked all night the field
breathed its dew until
the great gold ball of day
sprang up from the dark hill.

122

Now as the children come
the field and they are met.
Their day is measured and marked,
its lanes and tapes are set;

and the children gilt by the sun
shoulder one another;
crouch at the marks to run,
and spring, and run together—

the children pledged and matched,
and built to win or lose,
who grow, while no one watches,
the selves in their sidelong eyes.

The watchers love them in vain.
What's real here is the field,
the starter's gun, the lane,
the ball dropped or held;

and set towards the future
they run like running water,
for only the pride of winning,
the pain the losers suffer,

till the day's great golden ball
that no one ever catches,
drops; and at its fall
runners and watchers

pick up their pride and pain
won out of the measured field
and turn away again
while the star-dewed night comes cold.

So pride and pain are fastened
into the heart's future,
while naked and perilous
the night and the field glitter.

The Diver

The diver pausing on the tower
draws in one breath—
the crest of time, the pride, the hour
that answers death—
and down to where the long pool lies
marks out his curve;
descending light that star-like flies
from air to wave
as summer falls from trees and eyes,
and youth, and love.

Then from the rocking depths' release,
naked and new
the headfirst man springs up, and sees
all still to do—
the tower to climb, the pause to make,
the fill of breath
to gather in—the step to take
from birth to death.

Then, you who turn and climb the stair
and stand alone—
with you I draw that breath, and dare,
time's worst being known.

The Poet

Simplex Simplicior Simplicissimus
stood like a shouldering crystal under the sun
and changed its light into all the colours of love.
Great heavens, they said to him, look what you've done;
you've turned What Is into There's No Such Thing;
now we must turn it back. And the butterfly's wing

dropped at his feet and the bird sang business only.
Simplex Simplicior Simplicissimus
listened to what they said, bemused and lonely,
but being still what he couldn't help but be,
still flashed scarlet, violet, green, incorrigibly.

And though he is slain and many times over slain,
he is the one who dies to rise again.

Reading Thomas Traherne

Can I then lose myself,
and losing find one word
that, in the face of what you were,
needs to be said or heard?

—Or speak of what has come
to your sad race
that to your clear rejoicing
we turn with such a face?

With such a face, Traherne,
as might make dumb
any but you, the man who knew
how simply truth may come:

who saw the depth of darkness
shake, part and move,
and from death's centre the light's ladder
go up from love to Love.

The Morning of the Dead

I *The Meeting*

Out of the sky that is always astonished by dawn
move the enormous unconscious clouds,
blindly becoming, being, undoing their being;
like the clouds of sleep that want what they are and no more,
untouched by future and past.

That's how I went on my pilgrimage; that's how I walked
(changing, altering, sleepily under the sun of love)
with my hand in the hand of another, to look for a grave,
in the blazing day of a town in the far north,
among pale toppling stones.

And found, under the clouds of the mango-trees,
a thin dark muscular man deep in the soil,
shining with sweat, clay crumbed in his stiff hair;
a man in the service of death which is the service of life;
a man digging a grave.

"What are you looking for?" "A grave, sixty years old."
The grave of somebody dead long before I was born;
the grave of a man I had met as part of myself;
a man silenced by death but speaking still in my life—
my dark grandfather's grave.

But he was not to be found. He had crumbled away,
and the wooden tablet had gone and the rose had gone;
probably some other stranger was buried there now,
bone nudging old bone. But since I had come,
he and I met, in my mind.

He and I met; and the gravedigger dripping with sweat
(putting away a stiff in time for the Saturday racing)
gave us a twist of a smile. Sixty years old?

Cripes, it's a long way to come for a long while ago.
Why can't you leave him alone?

But in that sky that is always under the grave
he and I met, bowed in our sleep like clouds;
touched untouchedly; clouds that melt into each other;
shapes that need not strive, because their event is their truth;
found each other in love.

II *The Interchange*

It is the eyes of the dead that memory
most ponders over, seeing a rain of crystals
time-long carrying back to earth their vision;
the insect's towers of eyes; birds' light-filled circles;
the fierce or gentle looks of animals
that half-see meaning.

These reflect light more truly than pools or lakes
relating it to being in a new way,
till earth shuts on them and takes in their sight.
In them light generates some new complexity,
able to answer.

So earth is made of answers, the eyes of the dead.
All those old tribes, dark trees endowed with sight,
found new replies to night and day. Their glances
forged a meaning between man and creature,
creature and nature.

But meaning cannot rest or stay the same.
Meaning seeks its own unthought-of meaning,
murders and is murdered, travels on
into new territory past touch or sight—
is dark entreating light.

What drives us is the dead, their thorned desire.
Their eyes of fury, loss or melancholy

turn on us, light tantalizing darkness,
obscurity seeking simplicity
or midnight's peace.

So though I stood and said, My heart's a rose,
the wheel of life and death still turned. The dead
cry, Bear my children; follow out my thought;
live for me, since you wear my life. Their eyes
reflect no rose, no sun,
till the earth grows
into that perfect fruit where day and night are one.

III *The End*

Now all things thinned in perfect clarity
desire to rise in this pure resonant air
beyond themselves and take on purity
past reach of vision—only the essence there,
and that rejoicing.

Becoming seeks for being.
Learning desires so to transcend itself
that nothing's left to learn. Time seeks eternity.
The flesh continually works towards its ending.
Earth stares with all its eyes upon divinity.

Shape making perilous way from shapelessness;
sense budding where the blind rock knew no sense,
language carving all silence into meaning,
and motion taking up so intricate a dance—
yet all corrupt, all dying.

Time's not for weeping.
Time and the world press on. So take life further,
let the thin bubble of blown glass, the passion
of vision that is art, refine, reflect and gather
the moving pattern of all things in consummation
and their rejoicing.

For this is what the dead desire—their meaning.
"I was borne down; my work was left unfinished;
alive I turned to stone; my love was ruined;
ignorance, oppression, pain left my sight tarnished,
my world corrupt and dying.

Oh make me perfect.
Burn with a fire of sight the substance of my sorrow.
Take what I was and find in it that truth
the universes on their holy journey
watch with their eyes of fire. Illuminate my death.
Till all the dead stand in their essence shining
Time has not learned its meaning."

Poem and Audience

No, it's not you we speak to. Don't believe it.
The words go past you to another ear.
Does the look seem to rest on you, or you?
Regard it well, and see: it passes through.
It is not you we look at and we hear.

No, it's not hard to speak. This is an answer—
how blurred, how stumbling, we have bitterly known—
yet answer, to a question. Who could ask
so strange a thing, or set so hard a task?
We cannot answer. The voice is not our own,
and yet its tone's deeper than intimate.

And when, expected and entreated long,
the question comes, we cannot hesitate,
but, turning blindly, put all else away.
Searching ourselves in pain, we yet rejoice
that the implacable awaited voice
asks of us all we feared, yet longed, to say.

Autumn Fires

Old flower-stems turn to sticks in autumn,
clutter the garden, need
the discipline of secateurs.
Choked overplus, straggle of weed,
cold souring strangling webs of root;

I pile the barrow with the lot.
Snapped twig that forgets flower and fruit,
thornbranch too hard to rot,
I stack you high for a last rite.

When twigs are built and match is set,
your death springs up like life; its flare
crowns and consumes the ended year.
Corruption changes to desire
that sears the pure and wavering air,
and death goes upward like a prayer.

FROM
THE OTHER HALF

To Another Housewife

Do you remember how we went,
on duty bound, to feed the crowd
of hungry dogs your father kept
as rabbit-hunters? Lean and loud,
half-starved and furious, how they leapt
against their chains, as though they meant
in mindless rage for being fed,
to tear our childish hands instead!

With tomahawk and knife we hacked
the flyblown tatters of old meat,
gagged at their carcass-smell, and threw
the scraps and watched the hungry eat.
Then turning faint, we made a pact,
(two greensick girls), crossed hearts and swore
to touch no meat forever more.

How many cuts of choice and prime
our housewife hands have dressed since then—
these hands with love and blood imbrued—
for daughters, sons, and hungry men!
How many creatures bred for food
we've raised and fattened for the time
they met at last the steaming knife
that serves the feast of death-in-life!

And as the evening meal is served
we hear the turned-down radio
begin to tell the evening news
just as the family joint is carved.
O murder, famine, pious wars...
Our children shrink to see us so,
in sudden meditation, stand
with knife and fork in either hand.

The Trap

"I love you," said the child,
but the parrot with its blazing breast and wing
flaunted in the high tree, love's very beckoning,
and would not be beguiled.

Look how first innocence
darkens through shades of knowledge and desire!
—the bait, the trap, the patience! When the wire
snaps shut, his eyes' triumphant insolence!

"I loved it and it would not come to me."
Now love is gone.
Cunning and will undo us. We must be
their prisoners, boy, and in a bitterer cage
endure their lifelong rage.
Look round you. See, the chains on everyone.

Quick, save yourself! Undo
that door and let him go.

Cleaning Day

I carried rubbish down
until the house was clean,
cupboards scoured, shelves ransacked and bare.
High the heap grew;
I struck the match and blew
while the flame sulked against the idle air.

Sheltered, coaxed and fed,
slowly it caught and spread
till I could stand and watch its upward stream—

the gesture, the intent
spiralling, violent
dance that began around the core of flame.

Humble and worn-out things
put up their scarlet wings.
To new and pure sprang up the grey and old;
until a self-made wind
eddied within my mind
and drew it upward in a heat of gold.

O fire the poets know,
I kneel, I strike, I blow.

Eve to Her Daughters

It was not I who began it.
Turned out into draughty caves,
hungry so often, having to work for our bread,
hearing the children whining,
I was nevertheless not unhappy.
Where Adam went I was fairly contented to go.
I adapted myself to the punishment: it was my life.

But Adam, you know . . .!
He kept on brooding over the insult,
over the trick They had played on us, over the scolding.
He had discovered a flaw in himself
and he had to make up for it.

Outside Eden the earth was imperfect,
the seasons changed, the game was fleet-footed,
he had to work for our living, and he didn't like it.
He even complained of my cooking
(it was hard to compete with Heaven).

So he set to work.
The earth must be made a new Eden
with central heating, domesticated animals,
mechanical harvesters, combustion engines,
escalators, refrigerators,
and modern means of communication
and multiplied opportunities for safe investment
and higher education for Abel and Cain
and the rest of the family.
You can see how his pride had been hurt.

In the process he had to unravel everything,
because he believed that mechanism
was the whole secret—he was always mechanical-minded.
He got to the very inside of the whole machine
exclaiming as he went, So this is how it works!
And now that I know how it works, why, I must have
    invented it.
As for God and the Other, they cannot be demonstrated,
and what cannot be demonstrated
doesn't exist.
You see, he had always been jealous.

Yes, he got to the centre
where nothing at all can be demonstrated.
And clearly he doesn't exist; but he refuses
to accept the conclusion.
You see, he was always an egotist.

It was warmer than this in the cave;
there was none of this fall-out.
I would suggest, for the sake of the children,
that it's time you took over.

But you are my daughters, you inherit my own faults of
    character;
you are submissive, following Adam
even beyond existence.

Faults of character have their own logic
and it always works out.
I observed this with Abel and Cain.

Perhaps the whole elaborate fable
right from the beginning
is meant to demonstrate this; perhaps it's the whole secret.
Perhaps nothing exists but our faults?
At least they can be demonstrated.

But it's useless to make
such a suggestion to Adam.
He has turned himself into God,
who is faultless, and doesn't exist.

Remembering an Aunt

Her room was large enough—you would say, private
from the rest of the house, until you looked again
and saw it supervised by her mother's window.
She kept there, face to the wall, some of the pictures
she had once painted; in a cupboard she had carved
was closed some music she had wished to play.

Her hands were pricked and blackened. At the piano
she played the pieces her mother liked to hear—
Chopin and Chaminade, In a Persian Market.
Her smile was awkward. When they said to her,
"Why not take up your sketching again? So pretty—"
she was abrupt. For she remembered Rome,
Florence, the galleries she saw at thirty,
she who had won art prizes at local shows
and played to country women from her childhood.
Brushes, paints, Beethoven put aside
(for ignorant flattery's worse than ignorant blame),
she took her stance and held it till she died.

I praise her for her silence and her pride;
art lay in both. Yet in her, all the same,
sometimes there sprang a small unnoticed flame—
grief too unseen, resentment too denied.

Typists in the Phoenix Building

In tiled and fireproof corridors
the typists shelter in their sex;
perking beside the half-cock clerks
they set a curl on freckled necks.
The formal bird above the doors

is set in metal whorls of flame.
The train goes aching on its rails.
Its rising cry of steel and wheels
intolerably comes, and fails
on walls immaculate and dumb.

Comptometers and calculators
compute the frequency of fires,
adduce the risk, add up the years .
Drawn by late-afternoon desires
the poles of mind meet lust's equators.

Where will the inundation reach
whose cycle we can but await?
The city burns in summer's heat,
grass withers and the season's late;
the metal bird would scorch the touch;

and yet above some distant source,
some shrunken lake or spring gone dry,
perhaps the clouds involve the day
in night, and once again on high
the blazing sun forgets its course,

deep-hidden in that whirling smoke
from which the floods of Nile may fall.
But summer burns the city still.
The metal bird upon the wall
is silent; Shirley and her clerk

in tiled and fireproof corridors
touch and fall apart. No fires
consume the banked comptometers;
no flood has lipped the inlaid floors.

Naked Girl and Mirror

This is not I. I had no body once—
only what served my need to laugh and run
and stare at stars and tentatively dance
on the fringe of foam and wave and sand and sun.
Eyes loved, hands reached for me, but I was gone
on my own currents, quicksilver, thistledown.
Can I be trapped at last in that soft face?

I stare at you in fear, dark brimming eyes.
Why do you watch me with that immoderate plea—
"Look under these curled lashes, recognize
that you were always here; know me—be me."
Smooth once-hermaphrodite shoulders, too tenderly
your long slope runs, above those sudden shy
curves furred with light that spring below your space.

No, I have been betrayed. If I had known
that this girl waited between a year and a year,
I'd not have chosen her bough to dance upon.
Betrayed, by that little darkness here, and here
this swelling softness and that frightened stare
from eyes I will not answer; shut out here
from my own self, by its new body's grace—

138

for I am betrayed by someone lovely. Yes,
I see you are lovely, hateful naked girl.
Your lips in the mirror tremble as I refuse
to know or claim you. Let me go—let me be gone.
You are half of some other who may never come.
Why should I tend you? You are not my own;
you seek that other—he will be your home.

Yet I pity your eyes in the mirror, misted with tears;
I lean to your kiss. I must serve you; I will obey.
Some day we may love. I may miss your going, some day,
though I shall always resent your dumb and fruitful years.
Your lovers shall learn better, and bitterly too,
if their arrogance dares to think I am part of you.

A Document

"Sign there." I signed, but still uneasily.
I sold the coachwood forest in my name.
Both had been given me; but all the same
remember that I signed uneasily.

Ceratopetalum, Scented Satinwood:
a tree attaining seventy feet in height.
Those pale-red calyces like sunset light
burned in my mind. A flesh-pink pliant wood

used in coachbuilding. Difficult of access
(those slopes were steep). But it was World War Two.
Their wood went into bomber-planes. They grew
hundreds of years to meet those hurried axes.

Under our socio-legal dispensation
both name and woodland had been given me.
I was much younger then than any tree
matured for timber. But to help the nation

139

I signed the document. The stand was pure
(eight hundred trees perhaps). Uneasily
(the bark smells sweetly when you wound the tree)
I set upon this land my signature.

Snakeskin on a Gate

Summer's long heats slowing at January's end
I found by the gate a snake-slough; its dry scales
of horn blew newly-cast in the hot wind
against the hedge, ripped between stem and thorn.
I took it, shivering, and hung it on the gate-rails—

thinking it emblem, if emblems had been needed,
of a time of life like January, double-faced month of change,
that looking backward sighs for the dedication's innocence,
then turns too many pages, to find the end of the book.
But its touch was closer than omens: dry, cold, strange.

Dry with life withdrawn; cold with a desert cold;
strange, between two realities, neither alive nor decayed,
the snakeskin blew in the wind on the closed gate;
and I went uneasily, watching, for my life's sake,
for a coil of poisonous dark in the pools of shade.

Then at last I saw him, stretching warm in the sun;
shining; his patterned length clean as a cut jewel.
Set free of its dim shell, his glinting eye
saw only movement and light and had no fear of me.
Like this from our change, my soul, let us drink renewal.

Turning Fifty

Having known war and peace
and loss and finding,
I drink my coffee and wait
for the sun to rise.

With kitchen swept, cat fed,
the day still quiet,
I taste my fifty years
here in the cup.

Outside the green birds come
for bread and water.
Their wings wait for the sun
to show their colours.

I'll show my colours too.
Though we've polluted
even this air I breathe
and spoiled green earth;

though, granted life or death,
death's what we're choosing,
and though these years we live
scar flesh and mind,

still, as the sun comes up
bearing my birthday,
having met time and love
I raise my cup—

dark, bitter, neutral, clean,
sober as morning—
to all I've seen and known—
to this new sun.

FROM
SHADOW

Jacky Jacky

We see you still through a mist of sentiment,
Galmahra, Songman, born at a time so unlucky,
in your tribe's last days, and you the last of their poets,
and doomed to be given the nickname Jacky Jacky.

No one recorded the time and place of your birth,
but the white men had your country when you were young
and called it Jerry's Plains. For what you were worth,
they fed you scraps and taught you a humble tongue.

No one recorded the way you came to reach
Sydney Harbour from your country far on the Hunter,
nor how you came to be listed as thirteenth man
on the solemn Expedition across the water.

And what did you come to feel for Edmund Kennedy?
What was it looked from your eyes at your gay young
leader—
your gentle bottomless eyes—as, grave and polite,
you found a road for that heavy preposterous cart,
growing more indispensable as the way grew harder?

Faithful, was the word the newspapers used,
and the officials, raking the rags left over
from their hopeful Expedition so gaily farewelled,
the few starved bones and bits of harness-leather.
Faithful—the way these wretched blacks should be,
but seldom are—a model for your people,
who sit in their wurlies and mope and are ungrateful
for our busy invasion, our civilized example.

They too should love and help us. So we gave you
a special medal to be worn for the rest of your days
and fifty pounds in the Bank for approved expenses;
and we spoke of you with pleased uneasy surprise.

Yes, something, some faintly disgusted incredulity
clouded our commendation. How odd of Kennedy
to die on so black a breast, in arms so alien.
It seemed somehow to betray a lack of dignity.

But you, Galmahra? I try to see into your eyes,
as frank and dark as the depths of your Hunter River.
You loved him, certainly; you wept as you buried him,
and you wept again, when your own escape was over.

But why? I imagine you slowly gaining hope—
hope that increased as the Expedition failed—
knowing yourself at last the trusted guide:
hope that somehow your life-pain might be healed,

that the smouldering flame in your heart might meet his eyes
and be quenched in their comforting blue; that you both
     might ride
through a nightmare country, mutually forgiven,
black logical as white, and side by side.

Surely he would give some word, some confirmation
that you were now his treasure, his Expedition,
Since all the others were left behind, or dead?
He began to write—what message?—then dropped his head.

Over its burning weight you started to weep.
You scarcely looked at the grouped half-hearted spears,
while his heavy head burned in. Not all your tears
could put that pain out. It seared you terribly deep.

In Maitland Hospital, after, you felt it burning,
a red-hot weight; and cough as you might, it stayed
till the day, years after, when drunk as a paid-up drover
you fell in the campfire. Like an accepted lover
you clasped its logs in your arms and into your heart
and died at last of your unacknowledged yearning.

Songmen may live their song, if they are lucky,
and you were Galmahra.
    Or were you Jacky Jacky?

This Time Alone

Here still, the mountain that we climbed
when hand in hand my love and I
first looked through one another's eyes
and found the world that does not die.

Wild fuchsia flowered white and red,
the mintbush opened to the bee.
Stars circled round us where we lay
and dawn came naked from the sea.

Its holy ordinary light
welled up and blessed us and was blessed.
Nothing more simple, nor more strange,
than earth itself was then our rest.

I face the steep unyielding rock,
I bleed against the cockspur's thorn,
struggling the upward path again,
this time alone. This time alone

I turn and set that world alight.
Unfurling from its hidden bud
it widens round me, past my sight,
filled with my breath, fed with my blood;

the sun that rises as I stand
comes up within me, gold and young;
my hand is sheltered in your hand,
the bread of silence on my tongue.

Eight-panel Screen

Here the Sage is setting out.

A simple garment, cloth of blue,
is gathered in his girdle. Bare
head, rope sandals; seven lines
circumscribe him; that will do.
Now the world stands round about:
a path, a tree, a peak in air,
one narrow bridge beneath the pines.

Here's the Boy, three steps behind.

A cooking-pot, a sag-backed horse,
and his master's steps to tread
with a bundle on his back,
a tuft of hair, a stick of course,
rounded face still undefined.
As the Sage goes on ahead
the horse's rope takes up its slack.

Now the path begins to climb.

But the Sage still knows the Way,
sets his profile like a crag
or an eagle; meets the storm,
never waiting to survey
World in a moment's breathing-time.
On go Boy and stolid Nag.
Tao knows neither cold nor warm.

Now the path goes down the hill.

Steadily the Sage descends;
Boy and Horse go patter-clop
past the charcoal-burner's hut

where the crooked pinetree stands.
On the Sage goes striding still.
Droops the Horse's underlip?
Does Boy falter in his trot?

Now they skirt the mountain-brook.

Past the fishers with their rods,
past the children in their game,
past the village with its smoke
and the ploughman in his clods;
up again the path goes—look,
Boy is dragging, so is Moke,
but to Sage it's all the same.

How, Boy wonders, be a Sage?
How ignore such aching feet
only thinking of the Way?
Wisdom seems to come with age—
if it's wisdom to forget
Stomach's groaning yawn for meat
and keep striding on all day.

Round and round the stairways wind.

Cloud and pine-tree, rock and snows,
surround the Sage's sinewy lope.
Muscles strung to meet the steep,
how his one blue garment blows!
Boy is rather far behind;
Horse is leaning on his rope;
Even Sun sinks down to sleep.

Look! The resthouse, there at last.

Sage sits down to meditate,
moon accosts the last of day.
Boy brings water, stumbling now;
sees his face there fluctuate—

not so round. More sternly cast!
Patience and the endless Way—
these refine us. That is Tao.

Advice to a Young Poet

There's a carefully neutral tone
you must obey;
there are certain things you must learn
never to say.

The city may totter around you,
the girders split;
but don't take a prophetic stance,
you'll be sorry for it.

The stars may disappear
in a poisonous cloud;
you may find your breath choked out.
Please, not so loud.

Your fingers and hands have turned
into hooks of steel?
Your mind's gone electronic
and your heart can't feel?

But listen, your teachers tell you,
it's not to worry.
Don't stamp or scream; take the Exit door
if you must, no hurry.

No panic and no heroics,
the market's steady.
No rocking the boat, we beg.

What—sunk already?

Letter

How write an honest letter
to you, my dearest?
We know each other well—
not well enough.

You, the dark baby hung
in a nurse's arms,
seen through a mist—your eyes
still vague, a stranger's eyes;

hung in a hospital world
of drugs and fevers.
You, too much wanted,
reared in betraying love.

Yes, love is dangerous.
The innocent beginner
can take for crystal-true
that rainbow surface;

surprise, surprise—
paddling the slime-dark bottom
the bull-rout's sting and spine
stuns your soft foot.

Why try to give
what never can be given—
safety, a green world?
It's mined, the trip-wire's waiting.

Perhaps we should have trained you
in using weapons,
bequeathed you a straight eye,
a sure-shot trigger-finger,

or that most commonplace
of self-defences,
an eye to Number One,
shop-lifting skills,

a fibrous heart, a head
sharp with arithmetic
to figure out the chances?
You'd not have that on.

What then? Drop out, dry-rot:
Wipe all the questions
into an easy haze,
a fix for everything?

Or split the mind apart—
an old solution—
shouting to mental-nurses
your coded secrets?

I promised you unborn
something better than that—
the chance of love; clarity,
charity, caritas—dearest,

don't throw it in. Keep searching.
Dance even among these
poisoned swords; frightened only
of not being what you are—

of not expecting love
or hoping truth;
of sitting in lost corners
ill-willing time.

I promised what's not given,
and should repent of that,
but do not. You are you,
finding your own way;

nothing to do with me,
though all I care for.
I blow a kiss on paper.
I send your letter.

Australia 1970

Die, wild country, like the eaglehawk,
dangerous till the last breath's gone,
clawing and striking. Die
cursing your captor through a raging eye.

Die like the tigersnake
that hisses such pure hatred from its pain
as fills the killer's dreams
with fear like suicide's invading stain.

Suffer, wild country, like the ironwood
that gaps the dozer-blade.
I see your living soil ebb with the tree
to naked poverty.

Die like the soldier-ant
mindless and faithful to your million years.
Though we corrupt you with our torturing mind,
stay obstinate; stay blind.

For we are conquerors and self-poisoners
more than scorpion or snake
and dying of the venoms that we make
even while you die of us.

I praise the scoring drought, the flying dust,
the drying creek, the furious animal,
that they oppose us still;
that we are ruined by the thing we kill.

Shadow

I stood to watch the sun
slip over the world's edge
its white-hot temples burning
where earth and vapour merge.
The shadow at my feet
rose upward silently;
announced that it was I;
entered to master me.

Yes, we exchange our dreams.
Possessed by day, intent
with haste and hammering time,
earth and her creatures went
imprisoned, separate
in isolating light.
Our enemy, our shadow
is joined to us by night.

Joined by negating night
that counterpoints the day
and deepens into fear
of time that falls away,
of self that vanishes
till eyes stare outward blind
on one invading darkness
that brims from earth to mind.

Then came the after-image
burning behind the eye,
single and perilous
but more than memory.
When universe is lost
man on that centre stares
where from the abyss of power
world's image grows and flares.

World's image grows, and chaos
is mastered and lies still
in the resolving sentence
that's spoken once for all.
Now I accept you, shadow,
I change you; we are one.
I must enclose a darkness
since I contain the Sun.

FROM
ALIVE

Habitat

Houses and bodies:
both limiting factors,
shelters, educators,
subject to alteration
by the inhabitants
under their own conditions.

This house is over fifty,
built to modest specifications
(a Worker's Dwelling).
It began as four rooms
(cook, eat, live, sleep).
They're still the main structure;
the rest hang on them.

Before we came here
it must have been real.
Old neighbours remember
the first-comers.
Cloudy outlines.

Digging the garden
I used to ponder their remnants:
crockery bits, smashed bottles,
iron bolts, shoesoles,
lost toys. Once we found
a small porcelain plaque
enamelled with chrysanthemums;
worth keeping.

Not much turns up now;
their time's silted under.

When we first came
the house seemed too big,
then too small,
now too big again.
When I'm alone
it creaks like footsteps.

Houses and bodies
have memories, but forget.
Things drop through cracks.
Mice chew old letters.

You and I, house,
are in our fifties.
Time now to pause
and look at each other.

II

Remember the three-day cyclone?
You rolled like a wooden ship
in waves of violence.
The front rooms flooded,
the doors jammed shut
but we rode it out.

Remember the long heat-wave?
Wood cracked and shrank,
tank-water ebbed to the bottom.
Air itself seemed flammable:
we were scared to scratch a match.

We trusted you as sailors
trust ships.
Assaulted by altering seasons
your weatherboard walls
stayed tight, your galv-iron roof
shouldered them off.

But there are scars; wood-fibres
weaken; a little dust
sifts down, piles up.
Nails loosen.

III

An eight-foot carpet-snake
used to winter in the ceiling.
We heard him roll and stretch
when the evening fire was lighted.
He left each spring
on his own affairs.
Finally
some stick-happy farmer
took him for a trophy.
That winter the rats
came back.

The ceiling also sheltered
possums, mice, spiders.
A blossom-bat hung itself
neatly in my bedroom,
small fur umbrella
with live eyes.

Mud-wasps built cells
in hollows under books,
cicadas left horny ghosts,
split-backed, hooked to weatherboards.
The house was habitat
for things we never noticed.

Wood is hospitable,
even eatable,
subject to destruction;
the only stuff to live in
for destructible people.

Who'd live in steel and plastic,
corseting their lives
with things not decently mortal?

We're perishable, house,
but nourishing.
I too am hostess
for numerous inhabitants—
a rich bacterial fauna.

Symbiosis—
that's our fate,
my wooden house.

IV

Furniture: humble, dependent,
asking for nothing
except to be there, to be used,
to be let stay around,
like an ageing aunt
waiting to hold the new baby.

Once in a street
I saw two old chairs
put out for the rubbish-collector.
They were shamed; their patches and stains
like age-spots and tear-tracks,
their bony legs
thin and bowed, their laps
suddenly empty.

Furniture likes its own place,
wears its way into carpets.
Move it around, even,
it looks dispossessed.
People are all it has left
of forests, of living and growing;

which is why furniture likes us,
can be betrayed.

Mirrors: cool ones.
Too quick on the uptake
they've got all the snap answers before you.
They follow you round
and observe you.

They remember you instantly
like clever policemen,
and keep on reminding you
how you looked ten years ago.

Mirrors lie waiting in tombs.
Etruscan ladies
tried to take them along;
but glibly and faithlessly
they answer the tomb-robber.

They wait smooth and calm in the night
utterly certain
daylight will come back and find them
contemporary,
relevant,
quite up on the issues.

Mirrors repeat and repeat
that we're vain and ugly
but will always need mirrors.
Only the final bomb
will melt the last mirror
with the last face.

What will the last face
look like?
Mirrors know.
It will contain all faces, all

human history
(which mirrors remember).

Shatter them: every knife-sharp bit
is a mirror, cursing you
seven years long.
Even their wooden frames
wince back, sensitive
as fingernails clipped too close,
from their ice-blink.

Mirrors reverse us.
Mirrors are mathematics,
reason, logic.
They stare at each other and demonstrate
Infinite Regress:
Reductio ad Absurdum:
Eternity: Zero:
the Cyclical Theory:
Vanitas Vanitatum.

Furniture wears out and dies.
Mirrors
never.

VIII

Lit up, within and upon
darkness of air and ground,
my house, you stand
and darkness crowds around.

Guns level and bombs drop;
evil's come and to come;
eyes cock in the world's dark
for deeds yet to be done.

None of us innocent?
No; our light words hide

not one black dream
nor one imagined murder.

Guilt's our inhabitant
pacing all night inside
this well-lit frame.
Chaos incentres order.

Slow helices of smoke
signal up from the pit
our words contain,
twining within all reason.

We're bound for deeper dark.
I start up in my sleep
thinking it's dawn,
but that's another season.

Yet, dawns there were and are.
Hands, eyes, once interlaced
and can, and do, again.
Ride out the night, my house.

Some Words

Unless

Had a whole dream once
full of nothing else

A bottomless pit,
eyes bulged out
across it,
neck stretched out
over it.

A whole life I know of
fell into it
once;
and never came back.

Therefore

Three white lines
joining exactly,
all the angles
equal.

Inside it—
symmetrical
cross-legged,
one finger up,
expounding a simple fact
sits Nobody.

A perfect confined space;
not one star
shines in.

Enough

No use, we'll never catch it.
It's just ahead,
a puff
of flying light.

Want it! want it!
Wake up at night
crying for it,
walk round all day
needing it.

Till one day
it's there.

Not needed any more,
not even wanted.

Look at it without a smile.
Turn away.

Dialogue

All dialogue's a bargain:
while A supplies the words
B adds the silence.
Or here's the poem
set on a blank of paper;
the music's pattern
is eloquent only against its intervals.

So, sometimes,
half-lost in thought or reading,
I raise unfocused eyes.
Some luck of shadow
sets you in your own chair—
seen, not by will imagined,
simply because I need your silence there.

I half-start up, half-speak;
even that half- is made out of my knowledge
that you are gone. It comes
not from the time we spent together
but from the years without you:
the film's dark negative,
the silence after talk.

Your not-being's true
just as your being was.
It circles me, a lightless moon

seen by my light.
The years of unrelation
complete you for me.

All that I see says blandly,
"I'm Now, I'm three-dimensional;"
yes, but what else?
Concave backs convex.
Turn Presence inside out
Absence is demonstrated.
Flick off the conscious switch,
there's Nothing, sprung
out of its secret place behind the world.

So here's our dialogue
made out of plus and minus,
zero and number.
I play with world's this-side—
but did we ever find that smooth magician
much more than half-convincing?

Space Between

Space between lip and lip
and space between
living and long-dead flesh
can sometimes seem the same.

We strive across, we strain
to those who breathe the air,
to those in memory;
but Here is never There.

What is the space between,
enclosing us in one

united person, yet
dividing each alone?

Frail bridges cross from eye
to eye, from flesh to flesh,
from word to world; the net
is gapped at every mesh;

and this each human knows:
however close our touch
or intimate our speech,
silences, spaces reach
most deep, and will not close.

Two Dreamtimes
(For Kath Walker, now Oodgeroo Noonuccal)

Kathy my sister with the torn heart,
I don't know how to thank you
for your dreamtime stories of joy and grief
written on paperbark.

You were one of the dark children
I wasn't allowed to play with—
riverbank campers, the wrong colour
(I couldn't turn you white.)

So it was late I met you,
late I began to know
they hadn't told me the land I loved
was taken out of your hands.

Sitting all night at my kitchen table
with a cry and a song in your voice,
your eyes were full of the dying children,
the blank-eyed taken women,

the sullen looks of the men who sold them
for rum to forget the selling;
the hard rational white faces
with eyes that forget the past.

With a knifeblade flash in your black eyes
that always long to be blacker,
your Spanish-Koori face
of a fighter and singer,

arms over your breast folding
your sorrow in to hold it,
you brought me to you some of the way
and came the rest to meet me;

over the desert of red sand
came from your lost country
to where I stand with all my fathers,
their guilt and righteousness.

Over the rum your voice sang
the tales of an old people,
their dreaming buried, the place forgotten . . .
We too have lost our dreaming.

We the robbers, robbed in turn,
selling this land on hire-purchase;
what's stolen once is stolen again
even before we know it.

If we are sisters, it's in this—
our grief for a lost country,
the place we dreamed in long ago,
poisoned now and crumbling.

Let us go back to that far time,
I riding the cleared hills,
plucking blue leaves for their eucalypt scent,
hearing the call of the plover,

in a land I thought was mine for life.
I mourn it as you mourn
the ripped length of the island beaches,
the drained paperbark swamps.

The easy Eden-dreamtime then
in a country of birds and trees
made me your shadow-sister, child,
dark girl I couldn't play with.

But we are grown to a changed world;
over the drinks at night
we can exchange our separate griefs,
but yours and mine are different.

A knife's between us. My righteous kin
still have cruel faces.
Neither you nor I can win them,
though we meet in secret kindness.

I am born of the conquerors,
you of the persecuted.
Raped by rum and an alien law,
progress and economics,

are you and I and a once-loved land
peopled by tribes and trees;
doomed by traders and stock-exchanges,
bought by faceless strangers.

And you and I are bought and sold,
our songs and stories too,
though quoted low in a falling market
(publishers shake their heads at poets).

Time that we shared for a little while,
telling sad tales of women
(black or white at a different price)
meant much and little to us.

My shadow-sister, I sing to you
from my place with my righteous kin,
to where you stand with the Koori dead,
"Trust none—not even poets".

The knife's between us. I turn it round,
the handle to your side,
the weapon made from your country's bones.
I have no right to take it.

But both of us die as our dreamtime dies.
I don't know what to give you
for your gay stories, your sad eyes,
but that, and a poem, sister.

Lament for Passenger Pigeons
("Don't ask for the meaning, ask for the use."- Wittgenstein)

The voice of water as it flows and falls,
the noise air makes against earth-surfaces
have changed; are changing to the tunes we choose.

What wooed and echoed in the pigeon's voice?
We have not heard the bird. How reinvent
that passenger, its million wings and hues,

when we have lost the bird, the thing itself,
the sheen of life on flashing long migrations?
Might human musics hold it, could we hear?

Trapped in the fouling nests of time and space,
we turn the music on; but it is man,
and it is man who lends a deafening ear.

And it is man we eat and man we drink
and man who thickens round us like a stain.
Ice at the polar axis smells of men.

A word, a class, a formula, a use:
that is the rhythm, the cycle we impose.
The sirens sang us to the ends of sea,

and changed to us; their voices were our own,
jug-jug to dirty ears in dirtied brine.
Pigeons and angels sang us to the sky

and turned to metal and a dirty need.
The height of sky, the depth of sea we are,
sick with a yellow stain, a fouling dye.

Whatever Being is, that formula,
it dies as we pursue it past the word.
We have not asked the meaning, but the use.

What is the use of water when it dims?
The use of air that whines an emptiness?
The use of glass-eyed pigeons caged in glass?

We listen to the sea, that old machine,
to air that hoarsens on earth-surfaces
and has no angel, no migrating cry.

What is the being and the end of man?
Blank surfaces reverb a human voice
whose echo tells us that we choose to die:

or else, against the blank of everything,
to reinvent that passenger, that bird-
siren-and-angel image we contain
essential in a constellating word.
To sing of Being, its escaping wing,
to utter absence in a human chord
and recreate the meaning as we sing.

Alive

Light; and water. One drop.
Under the microscope
an outline. Slight
as a rim of glass;
barely and sparely there,
a scarcely-occupied shape.

What's more, the thing's alive.
How do I recognize
in a fleck so small
no human term applies—
no word's so minimal—
life's squirming throb and wave?

Locked in the focused stare
of the lens, my sight
flinches; a tiny kick.
The life in me replies
signalling back
"You there: I here."
What matters isn't size.

What matters is . . . form. Form
concentrated, exact,
proof of a theorem
whose lines are lines of force
marking a limit. Trim,
somehow matter-of-fact,
even matter-of-course.
But alive. Like my eyes. Alive.

Geology Lecture

"We need some knowledge of the rocks beneath..."
Oh yes indeed, oh yes, indeed we do.
The furnace of an old volcanic breath
survives and culminates in me and you.

"The Lower Paleozoic muds and sands
laid down five hundred million years ago
contain few fossils." Life's obscure commands
direct our blood, still salt from far below.

"Sea-lily stems, some radiolaria,
and vegetation unidentified..."
We feel complacent. How evolved we are
who stare down knowingly at lens and slide!

"The horizontal layers gently fold;
the sediments consolidate to shale.
The last Ice Age..." a reminiscent cold
shivers our spines as we absorb the tale.

"During the Cainozoic lava-flows
these ranges were built up." They wear away.
We perch upon them now in half a doze
sitting with gently folded hands today;

containing all prehistory in our bones
and all geology behind the brain
which in the Modern age could melt these stones
so fiercely, time might never start again.

White Night

The dream jumps me awake.
Earth's secretive dog, the moon,
grins sidelong through the pane.
Time's shallower than we thought.
Some meteorite's hot flake
rips blazing down, is gone—
or some sad manwrought metal?
We are tracked by our own evil.

The mind runs restless. Cast
back now, before time's done,
running head-down and thin
on the scent of the dying past.
Where does it all begin?
If evil has a beginning
it may disclose its meaning.

The hound sobs on the trail,
but the wolf's long dead—long dead
the unseen choice, the need
that led into this night.
Light-years of stars pour in
on to a sleepless bed;
the years fray, the threads weaken,
cloud crosses, corners darken.

"The boarhound and the boar
pursue their pattern . . ."
but what stars reconcile
the two before they fail?
What long chase closes in
to wreck what helpless prey?

Lord, it cannot be I!

Wedding Photograph, 1913

Ineloquent, side by side, this country couple
smiling confettied outside the family house—
he with his awkward faun-look, ears spread wide,
she with her downward conscious poise of beauty;
surrounded, wished-for, toasted by your clans
in the last threatening calm before the wars—
I look at you and wonder if I knew you.

Fathers and mothers enter an old pattern,
whoever they are; assume it for the children's
dependent and rebellious eyes. I see you
not through this amateur happy snapshot's sepias
but through the smell of a tweed shoulder sobbed-on,
through picnics, scoldings, moralities imparted
shyly, the sound of songs at a piano—

through all I had to learn and to unlearn,
absorb and fight against; through tears, then, better
remembered than through your love and kindnesses.
And she, pointing out birds or pansies' eyebrows,
gentle, fighting increasing pain—I know her
better from this averted girlish face
than in those memories death cut so short.

That was the most important thing she showed us—
that pain increases, death is final,
that people vanish. She never thought of that,
her second bridegroom, standing there invisible
at her right hand. Nor he of grief
whose laughing easy look was furrowed later
by private and public matters. He lived long—

so long, I knew him well. Or so I thought;
but now I wonder. Here in this photograph
stand two whom I can ponder. Let me join

that happy crowd of cousins, sisters, parents,
brothers and friends. I lift a glass as well—
the grey-haired daughter whom you did not know.
The best of luck, young darlings.
Go on your honeymoon. Be happy always.

Falls Country

(For Peter Skryznecki)

I had an aunt and an uncle
brought up on the Eastern Fall.
They spoke the tongue of the falls-country,
sidelong, reluctant as leaves.
Trees were their thoughts:
peppermint gum, black-sally,
white tea-tree hung over creeks.
rustle of bracken.
They spoke evasively,
listened to evident silence,
ran out on people.

She hid in her paintings,
clothed, clouded in leaves;
and her piano
scattered glittering notes
of leaves in sunlight,
drummed with winter rains,
opened green depths like gullies.

He took better to horses:
the galloping storms of hoofs
like eucalypts chattering
or stones hopping on slopes.
Enclosed in the dust of mobs
or swinging and propping

among those ribbony boles
he was happy.
His eyes were as wary
as soft as a kangaroo's.

Snow falling, the soft drizzle
of easterly weather
covers them, my old darlings.

What does the earth say?
Nothing sharp-edged.
Its gossip of lichen and leaf,
its age-curved granites,
its glitter of wetness
enclose them.

Is the spring coming?
Are there hooded orchids?
That's what their bones breed
under the talk of magpies.

Listen. Listen,
latecomer to my country,
sharer in what I know,
eater of wild manna.
        There is
        there was
        a country
that spoke in the language of leaves.

Reminiscence

I was born into a coloured country:
spider-webs in dew on feathered grass,
mountains blue as wrens,
valleys cupping sky in like a cradle,

christmas-beetles winged with buzzing opal;
finches, robins, gang-gangs, pardalotes
tossed the blossom in its red-streaked trees.

My father had a tale of an old neighbour,
the kind of reminiscence one inherits.
Asked for difficult detail in his stories
at those bygone ample crowded teas
(cup and saucer balanced on his knees):
"Madam, you might as well
ask me to enumerate the parrots."

Hundreds, thousands, birds uncountable
babbling, shrieking, swirling all around—
skiesful, treesful: lorikeets, rosellas,
lorilets and cockatiels and lowries,
Red-backed, Ring-necked, Orange-breasted, Turquoise,
Purple-crowned; Red-collared, Rainbow, Varied,
Scarlet-chested, Blue-browed, Scalybreasted,
Swift and Night and Paradise and Crimson,
Twenty-eight and Red-capped, Musk and Elegant—

I give up. But see him
sitting stiffly in a basket-chair
circled by their millions, formally
stirring three of sugar in his tea
in an afternoon I never knew
making conversation with the ladies.

Not a flock of parrots left to number.
Just a picture, fifty years behind,
left embroidered on my childish mind.
Parrots! They were something to remember.

Picture

So eagerly lightly the man
stroked his colours on—
the tawny sleepy slopes
the mood-dark mountains behind
and the fall and change of light
through clouds gentler than blue.
I stroke his hills too,
their bodies stretched in the mind.

Can only the young love
like this, with so tender a hand
and eye, see so
purely the earth's moment?
Past middle-age, I fidget,
pick at the years' callus
that cataracts my sight,
dulls my hand like a glove.

In what he paints I see
an earth I used to know,
light stroking slopes aglow,
earth various as flesh
and flesh its own delight;
and feel the young man stroking
his love, his earth, with a hand.
Time locks us up in the mind,
but leaves this window, art.

Grace

Living is dailiness, a simple bread
that's worth the eating. But I have known a wine,
a drunkenness that can't be spoken or sung

without betraying it. Far past Yours or Mine,
even past Ours, it has nothing at all to say;
it slants a sudden laser through common day.

It seems to have nothing to do with things at all,
requires another element or dimension.
Not contemplation brings it; it merely happens,
past expectation and beyond intention;
takes over the depth of flesh, the inward eye,
is there, then vanishes. Does not live or die,

because it occurs beyond the here and now,
positives, negatives, what we hope and are.
Not even being in love, or making love,
brings it. It plunges a sword from a dark star.

Maybe there was once a word for it. Call it grace.
I have seen it, once or twice, through a human face.

That Seed

That seed I took from a low branch
of a rain-forest tree
wore a red fruit like an apple
that might have poisoned me,

but I set and watered it,
waited day by day.
Nothing seemed to come of it.
I threw the soil away.

Now in the garden where it fell,
quite against my plan,
springs up a thing as stray, as fierce,
as tall as a grown man.

Should I take an axe to it?
Should I let it grow?
It will shade my window-sill
and choke the flowers below.

It will beat its wild arms
in winds against my wall.
It may smash my roof down
if storm should make it fall.

Damn the unexpected!
I don't know.
Shall I take an axe to it
or shall I let it grow?

Lake in Spring

The shallow reaches of the lake
on welcome-swallow days, lie still,
holding within a waveless blue
whatever comes, whatever goes
on path or hill.

So he and I not long ago
were there received and echoed back;
our living looks met eye to eye,
from calm and perfect surfaces
reflected to a perfect sky.

But now we move, we shift, we pass.
The images are overlaid.
The lake is driven by the wind
and stills again, and others cross
its mirror, and the world's remade.

Now when I bend to it again
another spring, another year
have changed and greyed the images,
and the face that lay beside
my own, no longer answers there.

There's little change in lake and sky,
they watch each other steadily;
but years took him and altered me.
Two look me back in this calm weather,
but who is this, and who am I?

A ripple goes across the glass.
The faces break and blur and pass
as love and time are blurred together.

Good News

Quite alone
I walk in the streets;
grey fume of cars
grey foam of clouds
savage south wind
ears like cold oysters.
Rejoice, rejoice
I say to the lot of them,
the end's
been put off.
A tiny crack
shows in the wall
of the grey jail
where maybe spring
has a seed waiting.

For awhile longer
my friends

can sing and paint pictures
can love and quarrel
and fall into despair
and come up out of it.

And you,
with sharks in your eyes
contracts in your hands
and balance sheets
that have to keep climbing;

you,
masks with false smiles,
bribers, connivers,
smelling of facts,
and factories
and underhand money,
short-changing the world,

and you saying I know
but you can't expect us
to do anything about it

we'll open a crack
in your grey brains
a fatal error
in your computers.

One crack in a grey wall
can spread,
one seed can grow.
Don't you understand
that a minute gained
might mean
everything?

Black/White

This time I shall recover
from my brief blowtorch fever.
The sweats of living
flood me; I wake again
pondering the moves of anti and of pro.
Back into play I go.

Had it been pro-biotics that they gave me
would I still live?
Antibiotics maybe snub the truth,
cheating the black king's move—
emptily save me,
a counter-ghost tricked from a rightful death.

But you can play on black squares or on white,
do without counters even; in theory
even the dead still influence what we do,
direct our strategy.
I'm none too sure exactly why I'm here,
which side I'm playing for—

but still, here's day, here's night,
the checkerboard of yes and no
and take and give.
Again I meet you face to face,
which in itself is unexpected grace.
To arms, my waiting opposite—
we live.

The Slope

Dropping my head between my hands I said:
Black vortices in matter and the mind

draw all things to their end;
all tissue capable of joy and breath
whirls on that slope and disappears,
and man runs down destruction like a hound.
"That's your true trail,"
cries the great Analogue of us all,
"You are the instrument of this planet's death."

The core of suicidal Earth
plotted them, then? That politician,
his grey look sidling like a rat?
These profitmakers cheating for position?
These muddy men too numb to know they kill?
These, the consummate product of time's will?
If you can believe that
cried my revolted spirit,
then die at once, you would be better dead.

Can you forget the ones you truly love—
poets and fighters with their eyes on truth,
swearing, like Thomas Traherne, so perfectly
to hate the dull corruption of their greed
that you had rather suffer the flames of hell
than be like these? Will you deny
the burst of glory in the world and man?

I call you up, true friends who lived and died;
my dead beloved, my guides, my living friends.
I say your names, I sing you to my side.
Keep far from me the sickness of despair.
Even on the last black slope
among mad images that rave or weep,
let all your voices call me back to air:
show me my true beginnings and their ends.

FROM
FOURTH QUARTER

Tightropes

Lacking in one capacity, you need another,
fair balance at the end of the pole,
to walk the tightropes. Some people
are unable to see horizons, but compensate
by concentrating intensely
on the next two steps ahead.

I've cultivated stability
by keeping my horizons straight.
Now of a sudden we're crossing
very mountainous country. The peaks around
draw my attention to the gulfs below;
I'm suffering from nausea. Dangerous for acrobats,
this upness and downness, the landscape running crazy.

Concentrate, woman, concentrate.
Free verse is harder to bring off than rhyme,
liberty than slavery. Remember,
the pole-end weight, the accepted convention
has dropped off.
Nor are you equipped with
an inbuilt spirit-level.

Late in life, though, to acquire the habit
long unadmired in others
of seeing no farther than the pace or two ahead
on a quaking rope.

Interfaces

I

Dreams: waves. Their wind-meandering changes
reach to the edge of shore, no further.
Their soft admonishing voices
sound from a sea where we can swim no longer.
Now we must wake. Whose heavy head
weighs down this shoulder,
whose hand this breast? My own.
The mist disperses.

Feed in the new day's reel
of punched instructions.
Sit up, pull back the curtain,
stop the clock's hectoring.

Out of the far-below
sea's fading murmur
one voice: there's more to say.
Wait, child; stay with me.
I would, I would, but time won't have it so.
Beached by the old betraying sea
I drag my body further,
crawl to my unfinned feet and dress and go.

II

Nearly all those sea-smooth rocks
on the southern beach where only fishermen went
looked like small whales. One was a small whale;
we learned that from leeward.

Walking round the decaying monument
we learned other things too.
The bared bone of the eye-socket

hollowed deep in. Like the temples,
transparent, withering,
of sad old people you love.

Whales tried the land early,
didn't like it. Easy to slip back
into the mothering upholding element,
be rocked again to half-sleep.

This is where they choose their suicides.
Dry harsh wind-battered beaches remind them
of an unaccepted challenge; their
old uneasy guilts
over that failure.

From the opposite direction, humans
come to their own extremes, remember
how they abandoned the faithful mother
to face a challenge they finally
couldn't meet;
and in a cross-traffic, take their own guilts
back to surrender.

III

Whales die of a sort of madness.
They choose their own beaching.
Watch them come in like liners
under deranged captains.

Try to turn such whales aside,
back to deep waters—
obstinately, blindly, certainly
they'll find another beach.

Death is inside the whale;
some diseased directive,
some inner treachery,
some worm lodged in the brain.

Afterwards, the whole air
of the coast's tainted
with an enormity,
corruption's total takeover.

You cannot bury the whale
in the beach it chose.
No sand is deep enough.
Some king-tide will uncover it.

Men must come, wearing masks
against decay's contagion,
chop it into small portions,
bulldoze it into trucks.

Far off, please. Very far off
where the smell of death can't reach us.
It's a huge task
to do away with a whale.

Whales are great mammals,
but no wiser than men.
Take the head, you scientists,
investigate its workings.

You may find, deep in there,
the secret of destruction,
the tiny burrowing worm,
the virus in the brain.

You may expound its reason,
but the whale's past cure.
It has finally rejected
the whale-road, the free seas.

If you mourn its choice, remember
not only whales have made it.
Whole peoples, countries, nations
have died in the same way.

Galaxies may be strewn
with staring burned-out planets
which took that path.

But this is to mourn a whale—
only a whale.

Half-dream

Half dreaming half awake
I felt the old boat rock at the lake shore;
small pulse of waves in the moon-road
slop, lip, withdraw;
pull and slack of the rope.
sigh in the trees.
Old boat
nibbles her rope, swings;
black swan stirs asleep.

Rise, fall of breath,
hesitant regular beat.
Tug on the wearing strand
all night long
sidling, slackening.

A peaceful dream. No sound
but leaf-talk, lip on sand,
shift of swan-wing.
Half-awake my heart
tested its moorings, turned
back to sleep.
Let the breath rise and fall,
the regular ripple and slack
fray at the strand.

Dream

A degree or two of fever, a dose of aspirin,
and somewhere past midnight
I think I wake from a dream.

So banal it was wholly convincing;
the clothes authentic, the set
three-dimensional, the cast and direction
faultless. The howling green hills of sea
storming the island and estuary
were quite familiar, attacking a country
whose map was clear in my mind. I remembered
everything as though I had lived there, though
I had never lived there.

A boring plot enough. First the Escape,
the door unlocked at dawn, the two,
trembling from hunger and torture,
waiting for the rescue-boat.
Then the Pursuit, the Capture, the Betrayal,
the roll of friends in the enemy's hands,
the Disaster, this time final.

Nothing retrieved,
the known world lost, diced away
among the inhuman powers.

I had been so entirely convinced.
Waking was such a relief. I almost heard
the parent soothing: it's all right darling,
you are perfectly safe. This is the real world,
and look, nobody's dying, nobody's being tortured,
the world is safe as houses.
Go back to sleep.

Obediently,
I lie back repeating

"No-one is dying, nobody's being tortured,
This is the real world and perfectly safe."

They

They look like people
that's the trouble.

Standing there at the door
leaning on the bar
shaking hands over the desk
they look like people.

Giving such a nice smile
a word about the weather
tickling the baby
shouting the drinks
even offering the isolated housewife
a quick pants-off behind the kitchen door
they look like people.

Only afterwards
when you're alone
you realize what you said
what the bargain was

you hear the click
as they say well thanks so much
and go off
to file the evidence

exactly like the click
in the telephone receiver.

Canberra: City and Mirage

The tawny basin in the ring of hills
held nothing but the sunlight's glaze,
a blue-blank opaline mirage,
sheep cropping, flies, the magpies' warble.
Burley Griffin brimmed it with his gaze.

Cloud-architecture in reflected image:
arena, amphitheatre, gallery
on gallery of quivering marble
rose from his mind – great circles, radials...
Over the clear-strung air his fingers played
conjuring a rhetorical opera-city
for that bald eagle, King O'Malley.

...Fantasies of power. The grey sheep nibble,
dogs snap at flies. Shoddy officials
argue his job away, confuse his plan.
Mirages, changed to lakes, lap sewage.
Cities are made of man.

The Dark Ones

On the other side of the road
the dark ones stand.
Something leaks in our blood
like the ooze from a wound.

In the town on pension day
mute shadows glide.
The white talk dies away,
the faces turn aside.
A shudder like breath caught
runs through the town.

Are *they* still here? We thought...
Let us alone.

The night ghosts of a land
only by day possessed
come haunting into the mind
like a shadow cast.

Day has another side.
Night has its time to live,
a depth that rhymes our pride
with its alternative.

Go back. Leave us alone
the pale eyes say
from faces of pale stone.
They veer, drift away.

Those dark gutters of grief
their eyes, are gone.
With a babble of shamed relief
the bargaining goes on.

Eve Scolds

Still so entrepreneurial, vulgarly moreish,
plunging on and exploring where there's nothing
left to explore, exhausting the last of our flesh.
Poor Natura, poor Eve.
Sungods are parvenu. I never could believe
that old rib-story you told.
You, to come first? It was Night, Water,
Earth, Love, I.
You Adam, son of the Sun—
you thought his maleness chose
you out of the unshaped clay

(his huge masculine beard, his dictator-hand
giving you strength). But I—
I *was* the clay . . . Little boys
have to invent such tales.
It's insecurity—always your trouble. You say
I nag you, hag of the night
drawing attention to your weaknesses.

But my trouble was love—
wanting to share my apples. You
called that temptation, put us both in with Him.
Not fair; I should have run home to Mother.
Now it's too late. I could never decide to leave.
Wholly bewizarded,
bullied, used as you use us, I rather liked it—
asked for it, no doubt.

But you and I, at heart, never got on.
each of us wants to own—
you, to own me, but even more, the world;
I, to own you.

Lover, we've made between us
one hell of a world. And yet—
still, at your touch, I melt. How can there be
any way out of this?
As always, I go overboard for you,
here at the world's last edge.

Ravage us still; the very last green's our kiss.

Eve Sings

These human words, this apple-song,
I take from our green world that dies.

I give them into your human hands,
I look into your human eyes.

Can it be we who grow so old
or is it the world? Poor world—
the worms in your apple foul and waste
the apple and the apple-taste.

Your second-Eden promises
fail like the first, though still we love.
Strain for one more essential kiss—
such greed and joy it's been to live
to the end of earth and all it was.

The knowledge was of evil and good.
We learn it deeper, growing old,
but cannot change our human mould
or nay the word the serpent said.

The apple's bitter to the mouth,
our last windfall from green earth.
The sword turns all ways and the tree
drops one last fruit for you and me.
I gather it for your human hands,
I look into your human eyes.

Builders

On great Ur-slabs of concrete terraces,
or rust-red bones of girder and cross-member,
they sit, eating their sandwiches
at noon. They look at home there
among the stylized trunks of metal forests,
the unfinished work.

Maybe the half-built is our proper habitat,
manhandling raw material
in basic contact, manipulation, direction
of various substances. Simple . . .

Later, the place changes.
Dressed in plastic wallboards, fitted
with doors and windows, connected
by cables, wires and pipes to the feed-in world,
it becomes part of a circuit.

Coming in later to consult officials,
sign papers, buy, sell, argue over contracts,
they observe the fake marble, the carpets
covering those bare encounters of concrete and steel,
the corridors scurrying with unfamiliar errands:
wondering. Wondering about building.
How whatever we construct gets complicated,
gets out of order and beyond control.

The Eucalypt and the National Character

I believe it is the casual informality of form, so much in keeping with
what one has come to regard as the national character, which has given
the eucalypts their unrivalled place in the Australian landscape, and in
our perception and consciousness of Australia.
(*O.H. Frankel,* UNESCO Symposium on Man and Landscape,
Canberra 1974)

Yes, we do perceive her as sprawling and informal;
even dishevelled, disorderly. That may be because
we are still of two minds about militarism and class-systems.
When we are informal, we are half afraid of bad form.
She, on the other hand, follows a delicate bent
of her own. Worn by such aeons, dried by such winds,
she has learned to be flexible, spare, flesh close to the bone.

Ready for any catastrophe, every extreme,
she leaves herself plenty of margin. Everything bends
whip-supple, pivoting, loose, with a minimal mass.
She can wait grimly for months to break into flower,
or willingly bloom in a day when the weather is right.
Meagre, careless, indifferent? With the toughest care,
the most economical tenderness, she provides for seed and
    egg.

Nor is she ever vulgar; she commits no excesses.
Her various gestures surround our pine plantations,
those fat green regiments that gobble our noble hills,
letting no light through, bearing no flowers. She is all light;
breathes in the noonday as lovers their lovers' breath.

She is artist enough to manage a graceful asymmetry;
but we are more apt to turn crooks.

For the Quaternary Age

When I looked down above the China Sea
on archipelagos of sullen pearl
and gaps of ocean flicked by sunlight's fin,
it set me staring downwards into me.

Quaternary Age that made me in your dream,
fertile and violent, swung from ice to heat
to flood to famine—what you've grafted in!
Could I be calm, when you are so extreme?

You tried to drown us in your melt of flood
and freeze us staring in your glacial step.
Burned by your intermitting fires I've known
splinters of crystal forming in my blood;

oppressed by shifts of rage and spells of calm,
I felt your lightning spread my limited skull,
setting me tasks no wisdom would have done;
thrusting in probes, filling the wounds with balm.

You teach apocalypse and hymns of praise,
the use of fire, methods of stone and steel,
sacrifice, surgery, physics, the worship of sun.
Bound to your flying heels we wreck our days.

Your unpredictable dealings drive us wild.
We haruspicate, compute and pray your weather,
retreat to hive in cities, foul nests of men;
but here in this dragon-shell I'm still your child,

adoring this sudden light, the gaps between
terrors, the glow of cloud-tops, crevices
of green serenity. Whimpering, half in love,
I press on the armoured glass to watch you, lean
to your diverse passages, asking what you mean
by those mute and merciful designs of pearl.

You knock me back with a fang-flash and a snarl.

Growing-point

A child in early spring, I stared
up at the sapling's growing-point;
a gathered strength, a total thrust
muscling itself, its swirl and sheaf,
to one high clench of folded leaf.

My body answered tiptoe there
a central need to rise as high
as limit, balance, let you go.

Around that axis spreads the weight
tree can afford by growing straight.

Breadth, form, completion—those depend
upon a proper symmetry.
The length of branch, the stance in space,
what leaf and fruit tree can sustain,
dispose around a central strain.

I knew no word for growing-point,
but in myself the sapling rose,
an aim, a need, a leap to air;
where weighted, rounded, bough on bough,
the tree fills out its limits now.

Encounter

Knowing too much altogether about beetles:
Latin names, classifications, numbers—six legs, four wings,
thorax, antennae, eyes, segmented abdomen,
I stoop, cut off his light like a thunderstorm
or bird of prey. My interfering finger
chases this hurrying black-clad person,
turns him over. Earthquake. This beetle can scream!
Heaving and bellowing, world turned upside-down,
he begs and curses. Given a stick to fasten
on, he clasps it, click, like a pocket-knife,
a mechanical clown.

After that mutual surprise
suddenly his whole shape turns to blur and buzz,
he's off, wholly at home in air, in life.

I've no idea what beetle is.
Beetle never recognized me. Nevertheless
it was a double event, a wild encounter.

Platypus

At midnight and alone
there's a stir in my mind
from a summer afternoon
very long gone.
A girl leant on a fence
watching a pool;
an arrowhead of ripples
broke its clear silence.

Platypus, wary paradox,
ancient of beasts,
like a strange word rising
through the waterhole's rocks,
you're gone. That once bright water
won't hold you now.
No quicksilver bubble-trail
in that scummy fetor

under the bank's worn grass.
No warm summer day
would bring a girl to watch
that current pass
for your wild shy head.
The pool runs thick
with car-bodies, cans, oil.
The river's dead.

But at this late midnight
suddenly my mind
runs clear and you rise through.
I sit and write
a poem for your sake
that follows a word—
platypus, paradox—
like the ripples of your wake.

The Marks

Suddenly seeing my hand—
obedient bored pen-holder—
there on the field of paper,
I notice that oblong scar
at the base of the right forefinger.
That one's the first I remember.

A three-year-old, related
to me by memory only,
tripped and fell on a rock
(or was it a piece of glass?
I forget the agent enemy).
The world went scarlet with shock
and shook with appalling noise
like the yell of a branded calf.

Sting of rank iodine, scream
of linen ripped for a bandage,
and over the blood and grief
somebody's careless voice,
"The mark might stay till you die."

Die? Die? Die?
Like a fly or a sheep? A word
to strike you dumb on a sob.
If dying is what will happen,
how shall I manage this trap
of a skin so ready to bleed,
and this hurtable bagful of red
in a world of sting and slap
and cut and knock and stab?

A long white line where the knife
slipped off a loaf of bread;
a nip from a blue mud-crab;
a scar from a barbed-wire jag;

a criss-cross pucker of burn;
a callus left by a pen;
a knuckle twisted by pain;
a random scribble of vein:

I have kept my skinful of red
on this hinged scaffold of bone
(with all due gratitude
to the help of medical science).
I have learned not to tumble down;
I can dodge and parry and hide;
I can handle kettle and knife.
It has been an enlightening life.

We have held off the enemy
and welcomed the friend and lover;
it has been a long alliance.
Director to employee
Hand: let's salute each other,
though the mark of each failed encounter
will certainly stay till we die.

Woman in Orchard

The woman in the orchard kneels
to love her body in the pool
and dream herself forever young.
Look up, you fool.
The witch's eyes are watching you.
She is what you will be,
hating what you are.

The peach-furred breast, the rufous hair,
the thigh's muscle, the heart's good—
that beauty's what the witch wants
and cannot have; and so she steals

not the flesh but the joy of it.
She has a quick wit,
knows what to get and how to get.
Look down, you fool;
the witch is watching from the pool
to make you what you will be
and poison what you are.

And who's outside the picture?
Look, look, you fool—
who but the man that painted it?
He sees the orchard-woman
and sees the witch behind her
casting the old and jealous spell.
Look how he brings the two together
in one reflection in the pool—
the ugly one you will be,
the lovely one you are.

At Cedar Creek

How shall I remember the formula for poetry?
This morning I have abandoned the garden.
Too overgrown to recall the shapes we planned
it flourishes with weeds not native to this country.

The thought of a calm wisdom, of manageable relationships,
of an old age with something to say
that any future will listen to
is scarcely reconcilable with the morning headlines.
Banking and Industry
welcome the big sell-out.
Report Urges New Approach:
Food or Famine?
Design for New Cities Condemned.
My desk is silted with papers:

Write to the Minister,
Protest torture of political prisoners.
Save the Forests.
Protest the Pollution of Estuaries.
Demand no High-Rise in this Area.

Where to look for the formula?
Complex ritual connections
between Culture and Nature
are demonstrated by linguistic studies.
The myths of primitive peoples
can reveal codes
we may interpret.
Gifts of women cement early political systems
assuring continuity.
Religions suppress the decays of time
and relate the Conscious
to the Unconscious (collective).
Metaphorical apprehensions
of the relations of deities, men and animals
can be set out in this schema.

Meanwhile keep lifting production for that is the answer
to inflation.
The rivers are silted already
here, and in Kyoto
I saw the sweet Kamo
choked with old plastic toys,
tyres and multiple rubbish.
The monks were singing
at the waterfall out of the mountain,
while shuffling in plastic slippers
we obeyed an ancient imperative,
which serves to keep cleaner
the floors of the temple.

There was a formula
under the willows of Babylon.
But the children have never seen Zion.

They condemn alike
our action and our inaction.
They, however, also base their politics
on the exchange of women
and speak a language
clotted with ancient metaphor.

One can only connect
between things already distinguished,
but distinction has taken us
a very long way from base.

Time alters the shapes of the garden
and introduces new weeds;
while "even a tiny change on the natural scale
can bring disaster
to countless humans."

By the waterfalls of Cedar Creek
where there aren't any cedars
I try to remember the formula for poetry.
Plastic bags, broken beer-bottles
effluent from the pig-farm
blur an old radiance.

For M.R.

All summer the leaves grow dense, the water-lilies
push up arrowhead after arrowhead,
burst into smoke-blue, hit the central gold,
and then retract themselves into bulb and mud.
Coming round the world, another season begins.

Martin, we have been writing to each other
for years, telling joys, griefs, happenings,
family gossip. Lives don't fit into letters

over one-half of the world. But talking over that space
we've been – what was it Plato said?—
happy companions in our pilgrimage.
You are English, Norman, Greek.
I battle that heritage
for room in another country, want to speak
some quite new dialect, never can;
it grows from my roots, it is my foliage.
Any time I flower, it's in the English language.

When all the living's done
it's poems that remain.
All that is personal, said Yeats,
soon rots
unless packed in ice and salt.
Poems can chill, shock,
stop you cold in your tracks,
functional as an axe.
But, too,
are a centring blaze in the field,
a sudden positive shape
sprung from the crowding leaves.

Reading your letters' news
I'd come on a poem. I felt
through the foliage of our lives
(and more than once is luck for any poet)
the arrow sprung to the target,
the shaft trembling in the central gold.

Envy

Envy, the artist's inescapable sin,
takes no account of difference, distance, space,
time, tradition, medium, age or race.
I want to have been in every hand and skin,

held every painter's brush and writer's pen
and sculptor's chisel. What a greeneyed pain
caught me staring at tigers in the temple of Nanzen-
ji last year! They were my tigers, mine.

But most of all it's reading poetry
makes me storm my limits like a jaguar's cage.
My hair and fingers crisp with jealousy
wanting this poem and that in hopeless rage.

If we've a heaven or hell, art's daemon will announce
to my arriving soul in either one,
"You can be—you are—whatever you envied once.
 What you longed to have done is waiting to be done

and all the boundaries are taken away.
You are Dante, Emily Bronte or Beethoven,
you can build the Taj Mahal, be Li Po or Manet.
Ask for a power and it shall be given."

Holding all skill and tradition, all times and eyes,
feeling the chill of the poles of art, the blaze
of its equator where the moment of making lies,
all lives and visions our own; past nights and days,

my raging kin, we'd shape eternity
into earth's image, make the unseen seen
in forms of immutable jade. What hell or heaven could be
our proper justice, envy's retribution,
or the reward of hopeless long devotion,
but reaching the highest power of what we've been?

Learning a Word

I can remember you, Tom Snow,
boy stalk-high as a telegraph pole.

208

When I was nine, a rhyming girl
testing words in a world too tall,
I found a new one: Hero.

You had a coarse but quiet face,
handing change in the post-office store;
you had a toss of wavy hair.
I took my bullseyes and a stare
in that small sea-holiday place.

It was a wild grey autumn gale,
they said, that broke the small boat's back.
The waves ran higher than the wreck,
hurling against the buried rock
a hull as suffering as a whale.

You swam alone to take a rope
out from the beach, like a long fish
towards the men who clung awash
watched by the anxious land. I wish
I could remember the tale's shape,

it was a year so long ago.
What I remember is that when
I came back, a girl of ten,
there was nobody called Tom Snow,
only a new word: Hero,

and somewhere a brass plate on a stone.
The small town watched the kingfisher sea
and the wind rattled the banksia tree.
Perhaps the thing was fantasy,
maybe I dreamed it, fitted on

a tale to a shouting hollow word
that sounded like the storm's black O—
a bubble of vowels rose and spread
round a dark and foundering head.
I rhymed the word with you, Tom Snow.

Counting in Sevens

Seven ones are seven.
I can't remember that year
or what presents I was given.

Seven twos are fourteen.
That year I found my mind,
swore not to be what I had been.

Seven threes are twenty-one.
I was sailing my own sea,
first in love, the knots undone.

Seven fours are twenty-eight;
three false starts had come and gone;
my true love came, and not too late.

Seven fives are thirty-five.
In her cot my daughter lay,
real, miraculous, alive.

Seven sixes are forty-two.
I packed her sandwiches for school,
I loved my love and time came true.

Seven sevens are forty-nine.
Fruit loaded down my apple-tree,
near fifty years of life were mine.

Seven eights are fifty-six.
My lips still cold from a last kiss,
my fire was ash and charcoal-sticks.

Seven nines are sixty-three; seven tens are seventy.
Who would that old woman be?
She will remember being me,
but what she is I cannot see.

Yet with every added seven,
some strange present I was given.

Moving South

"It will be cold where you are going."
Yes.
Working today in this sub-tropical green
summer extravagance,
cutting back fleshy stems,
smelling steam-scented gardenias
I think of winter.

Last night a chained dog howled
in the heat of the full moon;
the old house rustled
like constantly turning pages.

But far off southward
a stony ridge lay waiting
for me to know it. I move
closer towards the pole.
Wind off the mountain snow,
small white-etched trees
leaning in leeward gestures.
I shall step carefully into the acid vapour
of morning frost. At night
I shall light fires.

Doesn't summer
half know itself a cheat, conjuring
all this green foliage
to hide the rocks, the earth
that waits to take it back?
Beauté de diable
its enchanting flesh

already beginning to droop like an old breast
on ribs of bone.

I'm tired now, summers,
of cutting you back to size.
Where I'm going you will be more succinct;
just time for a hurried embroidery
of bud, leaf, flower, seed
before the snow-winds snip you
to a root's endurance.

I may be more at home
observing your quick passages,
stacking up wood
against the length of winter.

Unpacking Books
For Derek Walcott

On a dusty floor among piled rocking towers,
block-forts of prose, philosophy, history,
criticism, politics, sciences—word-cities
of civilization's greying geography—
I pick you up, poet of loves and pities,

and from green Caribbean nights again you sing,
This banjo-world have one string
and all men does dance to that tune.
Yes, yes, and yes, my blood answers,
takes up the tune and dances.

You too know the greedy fever's aftermath,
legacies of dead empires, the bitter taste
of warring faction, the natal land's slow death,
all energy, fertility, fruit ripped out to waste.

The rot remains with us, the men are gone...
Whatever we sang, dead politics denied;
the ruined rivers died, the forests died.
Yet poets keep an oath to hold and praise
what lives beyond the power-dreams of England, America,
  Spain.
Sweet naked Anadyomene drifts in to shore again
through oil-slicks, plastic discards, in our days.

Traherne said nothing had been loved as much
as it deserves. Though growing old I lament
too few answers to beauty's sight and touch,
too many words, I sit here now intent
on poetry's ancient vow to celebrate lovelong
life's wholeness, spring's return, the flesh's tune.

I twang that string again, rehearse the song
all ages sing, the dance I still remember,
taking a rhythm, a cue, a note from you,
player of violin and marimba.
There's an essential music still, a moon
where no man's landed, drawer of the heart
and muse of all our passion and our art.

FROM
PHANTOM DWELLING

Four Poems from New Zealand

1 *From the Wellington Museum*

Vine-spiralling Maori genealogies,
carved paths through forests
inscribed with life-forms, coded histories,
tangled my eyes,
never quite able to meet that paua-stare.

Outside the museum
(built, like the city, on a fault-line,
they keep on telling you)
the city climbs and scrabbles,
arguing with contours, trying to keep square.

Having dropped out of the sky
to get here, I knew the double fetch of oceans
belting a narrow land. Ridged peaking crawls
of alps topped neat with sundae-snow.
Surge. Pressure. Cracks of farmland
scattered with wool-worms,
sheepyards, wooden houses.

The city's only joke, winds tweak
hair into watering eyes.
Rain-blows whip up the bay.

A grizzled man, scotch-eyed, grey-overcoated,
stares from the terrace. A straggle of Maori boys
come swinging curls and tangles. Packs
cling like children on their backs.
Around his donegal-granite stance
their laughter parts, loops out
like water spiralling around a stone.

This sky flies clouds, gulls, ghosts.
Deep down, the world-plates struggle

in strangling quiet on each other.
Offshore, deliberate breakers hit the coasts.

2 *In the Railcar*

Gashes of wind on green-scummed water.
Gnawed terraces shelve the scoria hills,
the sea a hidden theme
beyond the dunes. Gorse, bracken, blackberries
scab over wounded ground.

Suddenly here an ancient crack of valley,
left to itself, its cloak of dark-green feathers
trembling with wind, drops down beside the rails.

Over the forest names
the Maori left, they have imposed
another country's history
(Palmerston North, New Plymouth)
Over the bared and crumbling hills
sheep eat, eat, eat and trot dementedly.

In small towns, tea-rooms
are called White Heather, Dewdrop Inn.
On rainy stations, pinkfaced countrywomen
drag children wrapped in wool.
Sometimes the soft-eyed long-haired young
run hand in hand, carrying hikers' packs.
COME ALIVE, the poster tells them.

Most birds in these square farmlands
are sparrows, skylarks, starlings.
Just once I see, hawking a narrow river,
one flash, kingfisher-blue.

3 *Entertainment*

Such kind uncertain ladies in their best
gather to entertain the visitor.

The local talent stands by the piano
fingering music-pages
criss-crossed with sticky-tape.
They sing "I Love You Truly"
to an audience in neat and nervous rows.
This district
"is essentially one of clean sentiment"
declared the Tourist Bureau publication.

The town, however, was christened
in honour of an Elizabethan playwright
whose sentiments were often questionable.
Much farther south
another questionable poet, Burns,
broods on another town.

Politely introduced, I lose my terror.
I read them Alec Hope:
Age. Passion. Loss, and death.

They lean a little forward. Faces answer,
"We too have not much time
to find the one in whose lost folds of hair
we long to sleep. Here too the early snows
have already fallen."

The single terrible white peak
rears in the window-frame.
It is for tourists. Just a tourist-mountain.
"But sometimes we too pause
and look, and look away."
So white, it casts a shadow on the day.

4 *The Beach at Hokitika*

A narrow shelf below the southern alps,
a slate-grey beach scattered with drifted wood
darkens the sullen jade
of Tasman's breakers. Blackbacked gulls
hunt the green turn of waves.

One girl with Maori eyes
gathers up driftwood for a winter fire.
But for her smile, the beach is bare.
I am a one-day stranger here,
not knowing even the gulls' language.

I hawk their beach too, looking for momentos
(as the souvenir shops wisely spell it).
A coppery log, a Maori twine of roots
—can't carry that.

Behind me, the sky's paled
by a swoop of mountains, scope of snow
northward and southward. Jags, saw-teeth, blades of light
nobody could inhabit. Not my country.
I go back to my loves, my proper winter.

Here in the chant of sea-edge, grind of shingle,
I choose one stone,
a slate-grey oval scrawled with quartz
like a foam-edge, an edge of mountains
white as my hair.

I take you this for love, for being alone,
for being itself. Being that's ground by glaciers,
seas, and time. Out of the sea's teeth
I choose it for you, for another country;
loving you, loving another country.

Smalltown Dance

Two women find the square-root of a sheet.
That is an ancient dance;
arms wide; together; again; two forward steps; hands meet
your partner's once and twice.
That white expanse

reduces to a neat
compression fitting in the smallest space
a sheet can pack in on a cupboard shelf.

High scented walls there were of flapping white
when I was small, myself.
I walked between them, playing Out of Sight.
Simpler than arms, they wrapped and comforted—
clean corridors of hiding, roofed with blue—
saying, Your sins too are made Monday-new;
and see, ahead,
that glimpse of unobstructed waiting green.
Run, run before you're seen.

But women know the scale of possibility,
the limit of opportunity,
the fence,
how little chance
there is of getting out. The sheets that tug
sometimes struggle from the peg,
don't travel far. Might symbolize
something. Knowing where danger lies
you have to keep things orderly.
The household budget will not stretch to more.

And they can demonstrate it in a dance.
First pull those wallowing white dreamers down,
spread arms, then close them. Fold
those beckoning roads to some impossible world,
put them away and close the cupboard door.

Late Meeting

The last, the very last
flower of the autumn
lifts its too-pale
head in the wind from the snows.

The last, the very last
journey from the hive
tempts out the wind-worn bee.

They meet, they mingle
tossed by the chilly air
in the old ecstasy.

As though
from this late take-and-give
some seed might set.

His dimming faceted eyes
reflect a thin
near-winter sunlight,

the gusts of wind
tremble her petals round him,
a failing shelter.

Brennan

Self-proclaimed companion
of prophets, priests and poets,
walker on earth's last fringes,
haunted lover
of the beckoning darkness,
last Symbolist, poor hero
lost looking for yourself—
your journey was our journey.
This is for you.

History's burning garbage
of myths and searches
sends up its smoke-wreath
from the city dump.
It stings in our eyes too.

Seeking in the flesh of youth
for Eve's spring meadows
of blue and golden flowers,
deep in their centre
you saw the empty question—
the question of the sphinx
half-nature and half-woman.
It mocked, No answer?

Walking the streets of your poem
you told dead Mallarmé:
here's your great book,
finished at the ends of earth.
it's the story of Man. Above you
in the black of Crown Street
the Cross's pointers
directed you in silence
to the pit of darkness;
the South Celestial pole.

In this continent, last-invaded
landfall of the Navigator,
full of survivals, Chimera's
final landing-ground,
you saw the Wanderer's
emptiest, loneliest desert.
On that stage, always pretentious,
you wore the solemn cloak
of old philosopher-kings.
Your ruined hawk-face
shone under your wide hat,
reddened with drink.
Your home was the black of Crown Street,
the kings being gone.

Lost dog of the end of a story,
black leaf blowing
in a wind of the wrong hemisphere,
you died before your death.

Smallest of stars, perhaps,
you cling in the pit of darkness
to the depth of Lilith's hair.

Victims

They are ageing now, some dead.
In the third-class suburbs of exile
their foreign accents
continue to condemn them. They should
not have expected more.

They had their time
of blazing across headlines,
of welcomes, interviews, placings
in jobs that could not fit;
of being walked round carefully.
One averts the eyes
from horror or miracle equally.

Their faces, common to humankind,
had eyes, lips, noses.
That in itself was grave,
seen through such a flame.

The Czech boy, talking,
posturing, desperate to please,
restless as a spastic trying
to confine his twitches
into the normal straitjacket—
what could we do with him?

The neighbours asked him
to children's parties,
being himself a child;
gave him small jobs,

having no niche to hold him
whether as icon, inhabitant
or memento mori.
He could not be a person
having once been forced to carry
other children's corpses
to the place of burning.

But when we saw him walk
beside our own children
darkness rose from that pit.
Quickly but carefully
(he must not notice)
we put our bodies
between our children and the Victim.

Absit omen, you gods—
avert the doom,
the future's beckoning flame.

Perhaps he did notice. At last
he went away.

In what back-street of what city
does he keep silence, unreadable
facing graffito of half-
forgotten obscenity?

Think: such are not to be pitied.
They wear already
a coat of ash seared in.
But our children and their children
have put on, over the years,
a delicate cloak of fat.

Seasonal Flocking

Last week outside my window
the tree grew red rosellas,
berry-bright fruits, the young ones
brocaded with juvenile green.
I said, the autumn's ending.
They have come out of the mountains
and the snowcloud shadows.

This week, on the road to town,
in the red-hung hawthorns,
eleven of the Twelve Apostles,
eight black cockatoos, their tails
fanned to show yellow panes,
uncounted magpies and currawongs
greasily fat from the dump and the butcher's throwouts—
that breeding-ground of maggots.

All of them flocked together,
crying aloud, knowing
the end of autumn.
Sharp-edged welcome-swallows
gathered and circled upwards.

Frost soon, and the last warmth passes.
Seed-stems rot on wet grasses.

At the end of autumn
I too—I want you near me,
all you who scatter
into far places or are hidden under
summer-forgotten gravestones.

For a Pastoral Family

1 *To my brothers*

Over the years, horses have changed to land-rovers.
Grown old, you travel your thousands of acres
deploring change and the wickedness of cities
and the cities' politics: hoping to pass to your sons
a kind of life you inherited in your generation.
Some actions of those you vote for stick in your throats.
There are corruptions one cannot quite endorse;
but if they are in our interests, then of course . . .

Well, there are luxuries still,
including pastoral silence, miles of slope and hill,
the cautious politeness of bankers. These are owed
to the forerunners, men and women
who took over as if by right a century and a half
in an ancient difficult bush. And after all,
the previous owners put up little fight,
did not believe in ownership, and so were scarcely human.

Our people who gnawed at the fringe
of the edible leaf of this country
left you a margin of action, a rural security,
and left to me
what serves as a base for poetry,
a doubtful song that has a dying fall.

2 *To my generation*

A certain consensus of echo, a sanctioning sound,
supported our childhood lives. We stepped
on sure and conceded ground.
A whole society
extended a comforting cover of legality.
The really deplorable deeds
had happened out of our sight, allowing us innocence,
We were not born, or there was silence kept.

If now there are landslides, if our field of reference
is much eroded, our hands show little blood.
We enter a plea: Not Guilty.
For the good of the Old Country
the land was taken; the Empire had loyal service.
Would any convict us?
Our plea has been endorsed by every appropriate jury.

If my poetic style, your pastoral produce,
are challenged by shifts in the market,
or a change of taste, at least we can go down smiling
with enough left in our pockets
to be noted in literary or local histories.

3 *For today*

We were always part of a process. It has expanded.
What swells over us now is a logical spread
from the small horizons we made—
the heave of the great corporations
whose bellies are never full.
What sort of takeover bid
could you knock back now if the miners,
the junk-food firms or their processors want your land?
Or worse, leave you alone to hoe
small beans in a dwindling row?

The fears of our great-grandfathers—
apart from a fall in the English market—
were of spearwood, stone axes. Sleeping
they sprang awake at the crack
of frost on the roof, the yawn and stretching
of a slab wall. We turn on the radio
for news from the USA or USSR
against which no comfort or hope
might come from the cattle prizes at the Show.

4 *Pastoral lives*

Yet a marginal sort of grace
as I remember it, softened our arrogant clan.
We were fairly kind to horses
and to people not too different from ourselves.
Kipling and A.A. Milne were our favourite authors
but Shelley, Tennyson, Shakespeare stood on our shelves—
suitable reading for women,
to whom, after all, the amenities had to be left.

An undiscursive lot (discourse is for the city)
one of us helped to found a university.
We respected wit in others,
though we kept our own for weddings,
unsure of the *bona fides* of the witty.

In England, we called on relatives,
assuming welcome for the sake of a shared bloodline,
but kept our independence.
We would entertain them equally, if they came,
and with equal hospitality—
blood being thicker than thousands of miles of waters—
for the sake of Great-aunt Charlotte and old letters.

At church, the truncate inarticulate
Anglican half-confession
"there is no health in us"
made us gag a little. We knew we had no betters
though too many were worse.
We passed on the collection-plate
adding a reasonable donation.

That God approved us was obvious.
Most of our ventures were prosperous.
As for the *Dies Irae*
we would deal with that when we came to it.

6 *Kinship*

Blue early mist in the valley. Apricots
bowing the orchard-trees, flushed red with summer,
loading bronze-plaqued branches;
our teeth in those sweet buttock-curves. Remember
the horses swinging to the yards, the smell
of cattle, sweat and saddle-leather?
Blue ranges underlined the sky. In any weather
it was well, being young and simple,
letting the horses canter home together.

All those sights, smells and sounds we shared
trailing behind grey sheep, red cattle,
from Two-rail or Ponds Creek
through tawny pastures breathing pennyroyal.
In winter, sleety winds bit hands and locked
fingers round reins. In spring, the wattle.

With so much past in common,
on the whole we forgive each other
for the ways in which we differ—
two old men, one older woman.
When one of us falls ill,
the others may think less
of today's person, the lined and guarding face,

than of a barefoot child running careless through
long grass where snakes lie, or forgetting
to watch in the paddocks for the black Jersey bull.
Divisions and gulfs deepen
daily, the world over,
more dangerously than now between us three.
Which is why, while there is time (though not our form at all)
I put the memories into poetry.

Hunting Snake

Sun-warmed in this late season's grace,
under the autumn's gentlest sky
we walked, and froze half-through a pace.
The great black snake went reeling by.

Head-down, tongue flickering on the trail,
he quested through the parting grass;
sun glazed his curves of diamond scale
and we lost breath to watch him pass.

What track he followed, what small food
fled living from his fierce intent,
we scarcely thought; still as we stood
our eyes went with him as he went.

Cold, dark and splendid he was gone
into the grass that hid his prey
We took a deeper breath of day,
looked at each other, and went on.

Rainforest

The forest drips and glows with green.
The tree-frog croaks his far-off song.
His voice is stillness, moss and rain
drunk from the forest ages long.

We cannot understand that call
unless we move into his dream,
where all is one and one is all
and frog and python are the same.

We with our quick dividing eyes
measure, distinguish and are gone.
The forest burns, the tree-frog dies,
yet one is all and all is one.

Notes at Edge

1 Brevity

Old Rhythm, old Metre,
these days I don't draw
very deep breaths. There isn't
much left to say.

Rhyme, my old cymbal,
I don't clash you as often,
or trust your old promises
of music and unison.

I used to love Keats, Blake;
now I try haiku
for its honed brevities,
its inclusive silences.

Issa. Shiki. Buson. Bashō.
Few words and with no rhetoric.
Enclosed by silence
as is the thrush's call.

2 Rock

I dug from this shallow soil
a rock-lump square as a book,
split into leaves of clay.

A long curved wash of ripple
left there its fingerprint
one long-before-time lost day.

I turn a dead sea's leaves,
stand on a shore of waves,
and touch that day, and look.

3 Fox

That rufous canterer
through my eye's corner
crossing an empty space of frost-red grass
goes running like a flame.

Against storm-black Budawang
a bushfire bristle of brush.
Under the candlebark trees
a rustle in dry litter.

Fox, fox!
Behind him follows the crackle of his name.

4 River Bend

What killed that kangaroo-doe, slender skeleton
tumbled above the water with her long shanks
cleaned white as moonlight?
Pad-tracks in sand where something drank fresh blood.

Last night a dog howled somewhere,
a hungry ghost in need of sacrifice.

Down by that bend, they say, the last old woman,
thin, black and muttering grief,
foraged for mussels, all her people gone.

The swollen winter river
curves over stone, a wild perpetual voice.

5 Lichen, Moss, Fungus

Autumn and early winter
wet this clay soil with rains.
Slow primitive plant-forms
push up their curious flowers.

Lichens, mosses and fungi—
these flourish on this rock ridge,
a delicate crushable tundra:
bracket, star, cup, parasol;
gilled, pored, spored, membraned;
white, chestnut, violet, red.

I stoke the fire with wood
laced with mycelia, tread
a crust of moss and lichen.
Over the wet decay
of log and fallen branch
there spreads an embroidery, ancient
source of the forests.

6 Caddis fly

Small twilight helicopter,
four petals, four skins of crystal,
veined taut with chitinous fibre
carry you into my wineglass.
Why such a dying fall?

I sat under leaves, toasting
a simple moon, a river,
the respite of an evening
warm as the hand of a lover.
Did you have to cry Alas?

I lift you out on a finger
dripping red with wine
to dry beside the campfire,
but you won't fly again.

All of a sudden
you gather four wings together,
still drooping, sodden,
and dive to the fire's centre.

Why should I mourn, little buddha?
Small drunkard of the flame?
I finish my wine and dream
on your fire-sermon.

7 *Glass Corridor*

Down the glass passageway
three of us walk. Left. Right.
And who's in the middle?

That's the lying inventor,
the self-contemplator,
with moonrise on one hand
sunset on the other.

We three walk through
a forest of tree-branches,
a swaying maze of gestures
eastways, westways.

Who knows which I am
this criss-cross evening—
or how many?

The Shadow of Fire: Ghazals

Rockface

Of the age-long heave of a cliff-face, all's come down
except this split upstanding stone, like a gravestone.

Sun-orchids bloomed here, out and gone in a month.
For drought-stricken years, I haven't seen those flowers.

In the days of the hunters with spears, this rock had a name.
Rightly they knew the ancestral powers of stone.

Jung found in his corner-stone the spark Telesphorus.
Earth gives out fireflies, glow-worms, fungal lights.

Walking here in the dark my torch lights up
something massive, motionless, that confronts me.

I've no wish to chisel things into new shapes.
The remnant of a mountain has its own meaning.

Rockpool

My generation is dying, after long lives
swung from war to depression to war to fatness.

I watch the claws in the rockpool, the scuttle, the crouch—
green humps, the biggest barnacled, eaten by seaworms.

In comes the biggest wave, the irresistible
clean wash and backswirl. Where have the dead gone?

At night on the beach the galaxy looks like a grin.
Entropy has unbraided Berenice's hair.

We've brought on our own cancers, one with the world.
I hang on the rockpool's edge, its wild embroideries:

admire it, pore on it, this, the devouring, the mating,
ridges of coloured tracery, occupants, all the living,

the stretching of toothed claws to food, the breeding
on the ocean's edge. "Accept it? Gad, madam, you had
    better."

Eyes

At the end of winter my self-sown vine sends up
sprays of purple flowers, each with two green eyes.

Driving home in the night I startled a fox.
The headlights fixed him staring and snarling back.

There's altogether too much I know nothing about:
my eyes slide over signals clear to the fox,

but what I do see I can fix meanings to.
There are connections, things leave tracks of causation.

The fox-trot marks in the hardened silt of the road
led to those chicken-feathers caught in the fence.

The fox's two green eyes echo his universe;
he can track rabbits better than I can foxes.

But I saw the chicken-feathers caught in the fence;
and fox, I know who's looking for you with a rifle.

You know no better than the two green eyes on the
     pea-flower
the link between the feathers and the sound of the shot.

Summer

This place's quality is not its former nature
but a struggle to heal itself after many wounds.

Upheaved ironstone, mudstone, quartz and clay
drank dark blood once, heard cries and the running of feet.

Now that the miners' huts are a tumble of chimney-stones,
shafts near the river shelter a city of wombats.

Scabs of growth form slowly over the rocks.
Lichens, algae, wind-bent saplings grow.

I'll never know its inhabitants. Evening torchlight
catches the moonstone eyes of big wolf-spiders.

All day the jenny-lizard dug hard ground
watching for shadows of hawk or kookaburra.

At evening, her pearl-eggs hidden, she raked back earth
over the tunnel, wearing a wide grey smile.

In a burned-out summer, I try to see without words
as they do. But I live through a web of language.

Connections

The tiny clusters of whitebeard heath are in flower:
their scent has drawn to them moths from how far away?

When I look up at the stars I don't try counting,
but I know that the lights I see can pass right through me.

What mind could weave such a complicated web?
Systems analysis might make angels giggle.

A child, I buried the key of a sardine-tin.
Resurrected, I thought, it might unlock the universe.

Picking up shells on the beach, said Isaac Newton.
Catch a modern physicist using such a comparison.

I can smell the whitebeard heath when it's under my nose,
and that should be enough for someone who isn't a moth;

but who wants to be a mere onlooker? Every cell of me
has been pierced through by plunging intergalactic messages,

and the cream-coloured moths vibrate their woollen wings
wholly at home in the clusters of whitebeard heath.

237

Oppositions

Today I was caught alone in a summer storm
counting heartbeats from flash to crash of thunder.

From a small plane once I looked down a cliff of cloud.
Like God to Moses, it exploded into instructions.

Home, a yellow frog on the shower-pipe
startled my hand and watched me as I watch lightning.

Frog, my towel is wet, my hair dripping,
but you don't for such reasons take me to be a refuge.

Small damp peaceful sage with a loony grin,
("one minute of sitting, one inch of Buddha")*

a long time back we clambered up the shore
and learned to play with fire. Now there's no stopping us.

Back to the drainpipe, frog, don't follow me.
I'm off to dry my hair by the radiator.

I can't believe that wine's warm solaces
don't help the searcher: the poet on the wineshop floor

was given his revelations. The hermit of Cold Mountain
laughs as loudly perhaps—I choose fire, not snow.

Memory

Yesterday wrapped me in wool; today drought's changeable
     weather
sends me down the path to swim in the river.

Three Decembers back, you camped here; your stone hearth
fills with twigs and strips peeled from the candlebark.

* Manzan (1635–1714)

238

Where you left your tent, the foursquare patch is unhealed,
the roots of the kangaroo-grass have never sprouted again.

On the river-bank, dead cassinias crackle.
Wombat-holes are deserted in the dry beds of the creeks.

Even in mid-summer, the frogs aren't speaking.
Their swamps are dry. In the eggs a memory lasts.

They will talk again in a wet year, a year of mosquitoes.
The grass will seed on that naked patch of earth.

Now only two dragonflies dance on the narrowed water.
The river's noise in the stones is a sunken song.

Skins

This pair of skin gloves is sixty-six years old,
mended in places, worn thin across the knuckles.

Snakes get rid of their coverings all at once.
Even those empty cuticles trouble the passer-by.

Counting in seven-year rhythms I've lost nine skins
though their gradual flaking isn't so spectacular.

Holding a book or a pen I can't help seeing
how age crazes surfaces. Well, and interiors?

You ask me to read those poems I wrote in my thirties?
They dropped off several incarnations back.

Dust

In my sixty-eighth year drought stopped the song of the
    rivers,
sent ghosts of wheatfields blowing over the sky.

In the swimming-hole the water's dropped so low
I bruise my knees on rocks which are new acquaintances.

The daybreak moon is blurred in a gauze of dust.
Long ago my mother's face looked through a grey motor-veil.

Fallen leaves on the current scarcely move.
But the azure kingfisher flashes upriver still.

Poems written in age confuse the years.
We all live, said Bashō, in a phantom dwelling.

Pressures

Winter gales, spring gales, summer—under such pressures
the contours of things crouch, their angles alter.

The sapling that yesterday cut this view with a vertical
today is very slightly leaning eastward.

Brown butterflies strike my window-pane.
When I get up to look they have always become dead leaves.

Gravity's drag, time's wear, keep pressing downwards,
moving loose stones downslope, sinking hills like wet
    meringue.

I move more slowly this year, neck falling in folds,
pulses more visible; yet there's a thrust in the arteries.

Blood slows, thickens, silts—yet when I saw you
once again, what a joy set this pulse jumping.

Winter

Today's white fog won't rise above the tree-tops.
Yesterday's diamond frost has melted to icewater.

Old age and winter are said to have much in common.
Let's pile more wood on the fire and drink red wine.

These hundreds of books on the shelves have all been read,
but I can't force my mind to recall their wisdom.

Let's drink while we can. The sum of it all is Energy,
and that went into the wood, the wine, the poems.

Logs on the fire burn out into smoke and ash.
Let's talk today, though words die out on the air.

Out of the past and the books we must have learned
        something.
What do we know, what path does the red wine take?

I cleared white hair from my brush on the dressing-table
and dropped it into the fire. Some protein-chains the less.

How long would my hair be now if all the clippings
from the salon-floors returned to join their links?

The paths that energy takes on its way to exhaustion
are not to be forecast. These pathways, you and me,

followed unguessable routes. But all of us end
at the same point, like the wood on the fire,

the wine in the belly. Let's drink to that point—like Hafiz.

Patterns

"Brighter than a thousand suns"—that blinding glare
circled the world and settled in our bones.

Human eyes impose a human pattern,
decipher constellations against featureless dark.

All's fire, said Heraclitus; measures of it
kindle as others fade. All changes yet all's one.

We are born of ethereal fire and we return there.
Understand the Logos; reconcile opposing principles.

Perhaps the dark itself is the source of meaning,
the fires of the galaxy its visible destruction.

Round earth's circumference and atmosphere
bombs and warheads crouch waiting their time.

Strontium in the bones (the mass-number of 90)
is said to be "a good conductor of electricity".

Well, Greek, we have not found the road to virtue.
I shiver by the fire this winter day.

The play of opposites, their interpenetration—
there's the reality, the fission and the fusion.

Impossible to choose between absolutes, ultimates.
Pure light, pure lightlessness cannot be perceived.

"Twisted are the hearts of men—dark powers possess them.
Burn the distant evildoer, the unseen sinner."

That prayer to Agni, fire-god, cannot be prayed.
We are all of us born of fire, possessed by darkness.